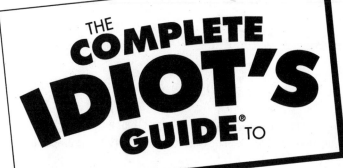

THE **COMPLETE IDIOT'S GUIDE** TO

Garage Solutions

Illustrated

by *Robert Russell and Theresa Russell*

ALPHA

A member of Penguin Group (USA) Inc.

To pack rats everywhere.

ALPHA BOOKS

Published by the Penguin Group

Penguin Group (USA) Inc., 375 Hudson Street, New York, New York 10014, U.S.A.

Penguin Group (Canada), 10 Alcorn Avenue, Toronto, Ontario, Canada M4V 3B2 (a division of Pearson Penguin Canada Inc.)

Penguin Books Ltd, 80 Strand, London WC2R 0RL, England

Penguin Ireland, 25 St Stephen's Green, Dublin 2, Ireland (a division of Penguin Books Ltd)

Penguin Group (Australia), 250 Camberwell Road, Camberwell, Victoria 3124, Australia (a division of Pearson Australia Group Pty Ltd)

Penguin Books India Pvt Ltd, 11 Community Centre, Panchsheel Park, New Delhi—110 017, India

Penguin Group (NZ), cnr Airborne and Rosedale Roads, Albany, Auckland 1310, New Zealand (a division of Pearson New Zealand Ltd)

Penguin Books (South Africa) (Pty) Ltd, 24 Sturdee Avenue, Rosebank, Johannesburg 2196, South Africa

Penguin Books Ltd, Registered Offices: 80 Strand, London WC2R 0RL, England

Copyright © 2007 by Robert Russell and Theresa Russell

International Standard Book Number: 978-1-59257-620-3

Library of Congress Catalog Card Number: 2006936706

09 08 07   8 7 6 5 4 3 2 1

Interpretation of the printing code: The rightmost number of the first series of numbers is the year of the book's printing; the rightmost number of the second series of numbers is the number of the book's printing. For example, a printing code of 07-1 shows that the first printing occurred in 2007.

Printed in the United States of America

Note: This publication contains the opinions and ideas of its authors. It is intended to provide helpful and informative material on the subject matter covered. It is sold with the understanding that the authors and publisher are not engaged in rendering professional services in the book. If the reader requires personal assistance or advice, a competent professional should be consulted.

The authors and publisher specifically disclaim any responsibility for any liability, loss, or risk, personal or otherwise, which is incurred as a consequence, directly or indirectly, of the use and application of any of the contents of this book.

Most Alpha books are available at special quantity discounts for bulk purchases for sales promotions, premiums, fund-raising, or educational use. Special books, or book excerpts, can also be created to fit specific needs.

For details, write: Special Markets, Alpha Books, 375 Hudson Street, New York, NY 10014.

Publisher: *Marie Butler-Knight*
Editorial Director: *Mike Sanders*
Managing Editor: *Billy Fields*
Acquiring Editor: *Paul Dinas*
Development Editor: *Ginny Munroe*
Production Editor: *Megan Douglass*

Copy Editor: *Keith Cline*
Cartoonist: *Shannon Wheeler*
Cover Designer: *Bill Thomas*
Book Designer: *Trina Wurst*
Indexer: *Tonya Heard*
Proofreader: *John Etchison*

Contents at a Glance

Contents

Contents ix

Introduction

The garage organizing industry is growing at a rapid pace. Consumers finally realize that the garage is a large space that is not being used to its full capacity. Well, some garages are filled to capacity with junk. This should come as no surprise, because it often is seen as the biggest closet in the house.

Just as closet organizing came into being, garage organizing has now grown rapidly with new products hitting the market on a regular basis. Franchises that cater to the garage organizing movement are springing up throughout the country.

Garage improvement has become more popular than ever as homeowners realize what an important part of the house it is. No longer is the garage strictly the domain of the male. Like the rest of the house, the garage is becoming more of a couple's or family area than ever before.

This book leads you on your way to making your garage a useful and efficient part of your house. We start with the basics and offer simple solutions as well as more complex options for turning your garage into a highly functional showplace. We feature several different types of products and instructions for improving the overall appearance of your garage. You learn how to repair drywall, install shelves, and build your own workbench.

Extras

Interspersed throughout the book and complementing the text, these sidebars provide pertinent information from a variety of sources. These tips by experienced designers, organizers, and installers assist you in every stage or your project and offer tried-and-true techniques, money-saving hints, and warnings that keep you safe and keep you from making common mistakes.

Definitions

What does that term or set of letters mean? Here and in the glossary in the back of the book you will find concise definitions of the important terms used in construction and storage solutions.

Drive It Home

These are practical tips and anecdotes from experts and garage solvers. These people have done what you are doing many times over. Their expertise helps you get it done right.

Loose Change

Find tips for saving time and money. When you are working on a budget and with time constraints, you want to know how to save money. Because time is money, anything that can cut down on the amount of time to complete a project is money in your pocket.

Warning Light

"Safety first" is our motto. This is where to look for common hazards and other pitfalls of doing the job. Besides keeping you safe, these tips prevent you from making mistakes that could sabotage your project.

Acknowledgments

No project sees completion without many people contributing along the way.

We want to thank professional organizer Diane Campion for her willingness to contribute her expertise, often fulfilling our requests on very short notice.

Feng shui practitioner Mary Mihaly stepped to the plate to interject her thoughts and wisdom on the principles of this ancient art as it relates to organizing, clearing spaces, and becoming free from junk.

Our son, Erik, rescued us several times when photos we were sent weren't recognized by our computer software. He helped with photography and seemed to know just where to find a car with a nest in the engine, a messy garage, or a freshly painted floor. He saved us hours of time.

Nathan Russell worked on building the workbench and photographed other critical illustrations for the book. During this time, he put on his contractor hat and did an amazing amount of construction and renovation on the house that we are currently rehabbing. He single-handedly took charge of everything involved, from digging out a crawl, mixing and pouring concrete, installing joists, and building walls.

Tatiana Russell supplied photos, sent faxes, and did other menial tasks for us. She did provide us with a place to work and stay in her house. She took the chaotic situation in stride while we skittered about looking for tools, photos, or overnight envelopes.

Many thanks to the different companies that helped with information on their products and provided us with some very fine photos and illustrations. Their eagerness to help us facilitated the project. Other folks were kind enough to provide photos of their homes, bands, and garages.

Special thanks to Paul Dinas, who remained calm throughout this rather intense process and during our frustrations and slow assimilation of technicalities.

Hearty praise to Marcia Turner, who helped with the technicalities of writing this book and offered her encouragement throughout. Thanks as well to Marilyn Allen and Gwen Moran for their unwavering confidence in us.

Final recognition to Jeff, who is always just himself.

Trademarks

All terms mentioned in this book that are known to be or are suspected of being trademarks or service marks have been appropriately capitalized. Alpha Books and Penguin Group (USA) Inc. cannot attest to the accuracy of this information. Use of a term in this book should not be regarded as affecting the validity of any trademark or service mark.

In This Part

First Things First

Has it really been five years since you last parked your car in the garage? Do you own four different #2 Phillips screwdrivers? Is that because you have one for different rooms in the house, or because you can never find one when you need it? Are you still trying to decide what to do with the six boxes of Uncle George's belongings that were given to you after he passed away?

Although garages are supposed to be places to park the car and store things, your garage could function in many more ways. You've already decided that you need to do something about your garage. We explore a variety of options and help you formulate and execute a plan to get you started on your way to transforming your space into your dream garage.

In This Chapter

- ◆ Characteristics of your garage
- ◆ The structure of your garage
- ◆ The size and style of your garage
- ◆ The contents of your garage

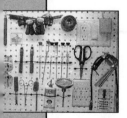

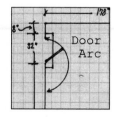

Chapter 1

Your Garage

Most homes have them. Some are home to the family car or cars. Others are home to all the stuff that doesn't fit in the house or the things that you don't know what to do with (or where to put them), displacing the family car to the driveway or street. Because you are reading this book, most likely you are not happy with your garage. Whether it is just a matter of organizing your gardening tools or a clean sweep of the junk, this book will help you evaluate what you have, what you need, and what you can do.

A Brief History

Garages evolved from the old *carriage houses* when the new carriages ran on their own horsepower and ownership of these vehicles started becoming popular. One car per home was the standard at that time. However, as society became more mobile and couples both began working, the need increased for more cars and for more parking space. These days, not only do Mom and Dad have a car, but so do the kids. Mom and Dad might even each have more than one car. In fact, the U.S. Department of Transportation statistics show that over 50% of households own at least two cars. The increase in the number of cars Americans own has resulted in an increase in the size of garages. The three-car garage is becoming more and more common in new homes. According to a 2005 Census Bureau survey, three-car garages are found in 20 percent of new homes. With garages already dominating the footprint of new homes, soon they will have more square footage than the rest of the house.

Besides being a place to park the car, garages have become the perfect space for storage. The popularity of bicycles, sports, and bulk purchasing has intensified the need for more space to store everything. The trick is to create a symbiotic relationship between your cars and your stuff.

Definitions

A **carriage house** was the spot to park the horse and buggy. With the advent of the car, the garage came into being and the carriage house often became a storage place. What goes around comes around.

The one-car garage was adequate when most families owned only one automobile.

Photo by Erik Russell

More cars and more possessions led to the two-car garage, which is the norm today.

Photo by T. Russell

Now that even teenagers have their own cars, garage sizes continue to increase.

Photo by Clopay

Anatomy of the Garage

Think of your garage as a large box with six sides. The bottom side in most garages is a concrete floor 3 to 6 inches thick. It may be level or it may slope toward a floor drain or toward the outside through the garage door. Some older garages have dirt or gravel floors. The top part consists, most likely, of a system of wooden beams, ceiling *joists*, that may or may not be covered by drywall or some other material. There may be a living area above, a storage attic, an empty space, or the roof *rafters* and roof deck.

Definitions

A **joist** is one of a series of parallel beams used to carry floor and ceiling loads. Joists are supported by bearing walls or girders.

A **rafter** is one of a series of parallel beams that supports a roof system.

The ceiling joists are sized for the *live load* and *dead load* they carry. In older homes, they tend to be spaced farther apart and are smaller in dimension.

Definitions

Dead load is the weight of the permanent components of a building structure that must be supported by the structure.
The weight of people, furniture, and any
other items that will occupy the building is
the **live load**.

The remaining four sides of your box are
the walls, one of which is dominated by the
garage door. This wall should be reinforced to
handle the additional stresses caused by opening and closing the garage door or doors. The
remaining walls may be exterior walls if the
garage is detached or they may be interior walls
shared by the rest of the house if the garage is
attached. They typically contain wooden studs
2"×4" or 2"×6" placed 16" to 24" on center.
Some builders use steel studs or build the walls
entirely of concrete block. These walls may be
covered with drywall or some other material,
and they may or may not be insulated.

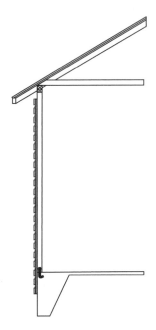

These are the structural components of a garage.
Photo by Robert Russell

Plumbing, electrical, and heating and cooling
components can be found in any of the walls
and in the ceiling and floor. Your garage may
contain active freshwater and wastewater systems that service a utility sink, laundry facilities,
or a bathroom located in the garage. There may
be pipes or other plumbing components, such
as water heaters, that pass through the garage to
other parts of the house.

Warning Light

Be sure to keep the area clear around
appliances in the garage that have
pilot lights. Don't store cardboard
boxes right next to the hot water heater or
furnace; otherwise, you might be cleaning
up after the fire department instead of getting the garage organized.

If your garage has electrical service, it will
contain wiring that supplies receptacles, fixtures
(lights or garage door opener), and switches
with electricity. Most wiring will run along
and through the wall studs and ceiling joists. If
you have a newer unfinished garage, the wiring
should be in conduit or armored cable to prevent an accidental break. If you have an older
unfinished garage, the wiring may be only vinyl
clad or even cloth covered. Should this be the
case, you may wish to consider replacing any
exposed wiring with armored cable or running
your existing wiring in conduit.

Your garage might have no heating or cooling components. It might have a single register
or it might contain the furnace and a substantial
amount of ductwork.

This garage has both a furnace and bathroom.

Photos by Erik Russell

It is important to know the anatomy of your garage as you decide what changes or additions you are going to make. Knowing where the joists and studs are (as well as where any plumbing, electrical, and heating and cooling components are) in the garage will help you determine where to locate safely storage units and other fixtures.

Modifying the mechanical systems to make the garage a more usable and efficient space may end up on the list of things to do. We discuss this in Chapter 16.

Individual Garage Qualities

Your garage has its own peculiar characteristics. It may be attached, detached, or even a carport. It might be a one-, two-, or three-car garage (or even larger). At the least, your garage will have one large door for the car. Typically, there is a door into the house from an attached garage. However, this isn't always the case. Our last home with its attached garage had no door to the inside of the house. Many garages have a door that leads to the outside. Many newer attached garages have a door to the interior of the home, one to the outside, and, of course, the main door for the car. It might have some windows, too.

Your garage might be built using wood or cement blocks. The interior wall might be unfinished with the studs showing or the concrete uncovered. The walls might also be *drywalled*, painted, paneled, or a combination of various wall coverings.

Definitions

Also called gypsum board, Sheetrock, gyp-board, or wallboard, **drywall** consists of flat sheets of gypsum sandwiched between heavy paper. The long edges of the sheets, which are usually 4'×8' or 4'×12' have tapered edges where joint compound and tape are applied to hide the seams. It comes in regular, moisture-resistant, and fire grades. Thicknesses vary, too.

The carport offers some protection from the elements.

Photo by T. Russell

This old-style garage door swings open.

Photo by T. Russell

The detached garage was typical in the early days of garages.

Photo by T. Russell

This looks similar to the old-style garage door but is actually on rails.

Photo by Elizabeth Edwardsen

The ceiling might simply be exposed beams or it could be finished. Perhaps there is an attic overhead. The floor of your garage could be dirt or finished. Maybe you have a carpet, tile, or another finish on the floor. Maybe you simply have a carport.

The garage doors are most likely sections sliding up and down on a rail; although if you have older garage doors, they may slide sideways, pivot, or open outward. Garage doors are made with a variety of materials from wood to fiberboard to steel, fiberglass, or composite materials. Although some doors are still opened manually, many garage doors have an opener or a touchpad for entering or letting others enter.

Garage Type

As you know, the garage evolved from the carriage house when cars replaced horses. More and more garages were built as the price of the car became more and more affordable. The detached garage was the first type of garage, following the model of the carriage house. In the 1970s, the attached garage became all the rage. Now garages are growing in size from those original detached one-car models to super-fancy three-car garages. Even though the types of garages aren't extreme, there are lots of varieties.

The carriage house was originally for storing the family buggy.

Photo by Clopay

The detached garage replaced the carriage house.

Photo by John Rider

Garages get bigger all the time because families own more than one car and often more than two.

Photo by Mary Mihaly

The one-car garage at Theresa's midwestern childhood home had double doors that swung out to open, a dirt floor, and a flat roof. Robert had a carport in his Southern home. Attached garages saved one wall of building materials because it was built right onto the house. One of our homes had an attached garage but with no entrance directly into the house.

Some detached garages on older homes have *porte cochères* or covered walkways separating them from the entry to the house. Today's carport is similar to what a porte cochère was—a protected area for getting in and out of the vehicle. Our old unattached garage had an outlet with cloth-covered electrical service, which didn't work. Some detached garages have no electricity, but rely only on natural light. Nighttime walks from the garage to the house could be rather creepy.

ABC Definitions

Originally a covered driveway for carriages, a **porte cochère** protected passengers from the elements. Some older homes still have this feature. Today, think of the covered area on funeral homes or the drive-thru at the bank.

Garages typically are built with the same exterior surface as the house, which is more of a consideration for a detached garage. A brick garage usually comes with a brick house.

The garage is a significant area of the footprint of the house and takes up much of the visual space. Front-loading, side-loading, or rear-loading styles are typical for attached garages. The particular style has a dramatic effect on the appearance of the house.

Front loaders have conspicuous doors, but are easy to maneuver into and out of. Side loaders need extra space for negotiating the car into the entrance. Rear loaders make the garage door invisible from the street, but need more space for swinging the car into its space.

The front-loading garage is popular, especially on small lots.

Photo by Robert Russell

Some older homes still have the covered areas where buggies dropped off their passengers.

Photo by T. Russell

The garage complements the style of the house.

Photo by Elizabeth Edwardsen

These garages in the same neighborhood match the style of the houses that they belong to.

Photo by T. Russell

The side-loading garage allows a nicer house façade but requires a larger lot.

Photo by Robert Russell

Garage Size

Garage sizes aren't really standard. Although the minimum for a one-car garage should be 10'×20' and the minimum for a two-car garage should be 18'×20', there are undersized garages, oversized garages, and everything in between.

Two-car garages are typical in new homes.

Photo by Erik Russell

> ### Drive It Home
>
> Although there are minimum sizes for each type of garage, there really is no standard size for a garage. Don't assume that your garage is a certain size just because it is called a one- or two-car garage. Measure it to know exactly the size you have.

Many garages have a significant amount of extra space in them, but not enough room to park an additional car, and so get the "half" designation.

This doesn't necessarily mean that the garage has yet another half of the space for the car or cars. Some have just an extra bit of space, and others have lots of extra space. This bonus amount of space means you have a lot more to work with and more flexibility in your plans. The undersized garage doesn't offer the same options as a larger garage. Don't worry. There are solutions for every size garage.

Making a Grand Entrance

You might be one of the many people with an attached garage who uses the door as the main entry into your house. It especially makes sense if you have a garage door opener that closes the door or a touchpad for entry into the garage. Logically, you just go into the house directly from the garage. If you still open and close the door manually, you may walk out to the front of the house and then enter your home directly through the front door.

The car takes up most of the garage, but there is space on the sides and in front of it.

Photo by the Accessories Group

A large percentage of homeowners with automatic garage door openers use the garage door as the main entrance to their house.

Photo by Erik Russell

Regardless of where you are entering your house from the garage, think about the impression that particular entry makes. Is it a welcoming and well-thought-out entrance with a place to wipe feet, leave boots, and hang coats, umbrellas, or hats? Is there a place for the car keys? Considering that your garage door might be the main entrance to your house, you might want to consider making it look like a main entrance. That means keeping the path to it clear of obstructions.

Warning Light _____

Detached garages and older attached garages may not meet current-day construction standards. They may have been constructed with substandard materials or inadequate spacing between studs and joists.

What's in Your Garage?

The garage morphed from the carriage house into the prime parking spot for the car, but many people never park a car in the garage. For some, the garage has become a prime storage space for everything that doesn't fit in the house.

Clear the clutter.

Photo by Erik Russell

For others, it is a work area. Think about Steve Jobs and others who started successful businesses from their garages. You need to consider the best use for your garage.

Drive It Home _____

Feng shui is about freely flowing energy. One feng shui principle says that every pile signifies part of your life that's "stuck." Clutter blocks new possibilities!

If storage is the best use for your situation, that is great. But if you just toss anything willy-nilly in the garage, you might want to ask yourself whether you are really using this space in the most efficient manner. Maybe you need some organizational help. We talk about getting expert help in Chapter 4.

The Cars in Your Garage

If you are using your garage for some reason other than for parking the car, you might want to think again. There are many benefits of parking the car in the garage, including discouraging theft. Although we keep our cars in the garage to prevent embarrassment, say that you do have one of those extra-fancy cars that you paid more for than a small house would cost.

Keeping your car in the garage eliminates surprises like this.

Photo by Tatiana Russell

No animal could have made a nest in this car if it had been in a sealed garage.

Photo by Erik Russell

A nice, neat, functional garage is your ultimate goal.

Photo by Rand Ruland

The elements, whether heat or cold, wreak havoc on automobiles. Sun fades the paint and the interior and can turn your car into an Easy Bake oven. The cold on the other hand might come with snow and ice that is oh so fun to scrape off. Even worse is ice everywhere. Think of how nice it would be to walk out into the garage to a relatively warm car in the depths of winter without having to plod through a foot of snow to get to it. You won't track as much snow into your car if you enter from the garage. You won't track as much snow into the house if you enter the house from a garage with a nice mat for stomping off snow.

> **Loose Change**
>
> Think about all the time you will save before work if you don't have to worry about scraping ice and snow off your car.

Some neighborhoods require you to put your cars in the garage and may bring you to neighborhood court and levy a fine for not doing that. If you live in one of these neighborhoods and like to change your own oil or do your own maintenance or just like to tinker, you need a space in the garage for working on the car. It is so much easier to carry groceries directly from the car into the house.

Rodents and pests are less likely to move into a garage and live in your car than they are if you keep your car out in the driveway. This is a real concern in rural areas.

Everything Else in Your Garage

If your car isn't in the garage and it isn't just a big empty space, it is likely that there are other things in your garage: tools, toys, sports equipment, boxes of unknown items, pool equipment, yard and garden equipment, seasonal things, car restoration projects, and more.

Once again, it is up to you to decide what the best use of this space is. And we can help you do that.

The Least You Need to Know

- ◆ Garages come in all shapes and sizes.
- ◆ All garages have common structural elements.
- ◆ Older garages may not be up to current standards.
- ◆ Newer garages are larger and offer more options.

In This Chapter

- ◆ Empty your garage
- ◆ Start thinking about safety
- ◆ Make some simple improvements
- ◆ Consider some elaborate storage systems
- ◆ Use your garage for more than parking the car

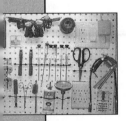  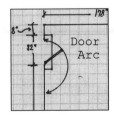   

Chapter 2

Some Options to Consider

We've talked about the characteristics, structure, size, style, and contents of your garage. You are probably ready to figure out what you want to do with your garage, if you don't know already. In this chapter, we try to broaden the possibilities of what you could do with your garage, some basic and some more grand. In the next chapter, we get more focused on what your dreams are for your space and what is possible.

The first thing to do, though, is to clear out the garage so you know what you have in it, get an idea of what features you might need, and what your garage really looks like without all the stuff.

A Good, Thorough Clearing Out

You might know what is in your garage, but do you know where it is? Clearing out the garage is the place to start on your venture to improving the space. You should keep the garage just as clean as you would any other room in your house. Could you imagine if your living room was full of boxes, tools, toys, or sports equipment, among other things?

Besides clearing things out just for the sake of organization, clearing things out can make the area less of a fire hazard. Piles of cardboard boxes stacked to the ceiling could ignite from a stray match, a spark from faulty wiring, or an accidental chemical spill. Storing solvents, cleaners, and gas improperly could easily contribute to a dangerous situation. If your junk is too close to an appliance with a pilot light, a calamity is just waiting to happen. With better organization, these problems can be eliminated.

Warning Light _____

You probably store gasoline for your lawn mower or other equipment in your garage. Remember that gasoline is extremely dangerous if not properly stored. Be sure to use approved containers and don't store more than the recommended amount in your garage. Do not use gasoline for any other purpose than as a fuel. It should not be used to start the grill or as a cleaning solvent. Check with your local fire department for storage restrictions.

GarageTek and the Home Safety Council conducted a survey and found Americans store many dangerous items in their garage. The following is a list of the top six. Are any of these things in your garage? Are they properly and safely stored?

1. Tools or sharp objects
2. Lawn-care products
3. Automotive fluids
4. Paint, paint thinner
5. Cleaning products
6. Gasoline/propane

If that doesn't make you think twice, then consider what else they found in the study. While only a quarter of the respondents were concerned about slips and falls in the garage, a third of them admitted to having had an accident in the garage. The Home Safety Council reports that slips and falls are the number-one cause of injury and death in the home. Over 75 percent of injuries that occurred in the garage were caused by tripping, slipping, or stepping on something left lying on the floor. Obviously, keeping the floor clear lessens the chances of an accident, and good lighting makes it easy to see any obstructions in the garage.

Safety isn't the only reason to get the excess stuff out of your garage. Clearing out the garage also helps you see any problems there might be. Maybe you didn't notice the water stains creeping up the drywall because the cartop carrier has been blocking that view for years.

Things touching the floor make a good nest for rodents or insects. It's not pleasant thinking about mice living in your box of quilting supplies or bees living inside that old garden tiller. Any dampness on the floor also can affect whatever is touching the damp area. In other words, move the stuff out and off the floor.

Warning Light _____

If you find insects or rodents in the garage, use caution with any sprays or poisons. They can easily be tracked into the house or enter the ventilation system in an attached garage.

This garage is a rodent's dream.

Photo by Erik Russell

This is a person's dream garage.

Photo by Rand Ruland

Quick and Easy Fixes

Everything need not be complicated, expensive, or time-consuming. Some improvements can take just a few minutes of your time, but give long-lasting results while quickly solving a problem. A leaky spot on the roof might require just a small patch. Now you can use that damp area you were avoiding before. The oil stains on the floor are a matter of simple cleaning. You don't need to risk a slip and fall while walking across the slick floor. That rake that wouldn't stand up along the wall needs a clamp to hold it on the wall or a closet to put it in.

This is an attractive way to store things with handles.

Photo by Alligator Board

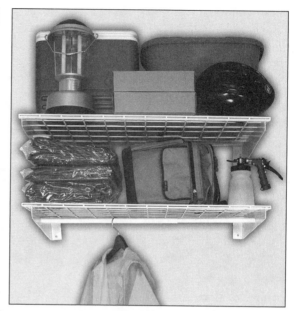

A shelf is a quick way to add extra storage.

Photo by Hyloft

$ Loose Change

Replace your garage lights with the new energy-saving mini fluorescent bulbs. These last much longer so you won't have to bother replacing them as frequently as the regular incandescent bulbs.

Other easy fixes include replacing burned-out light bulbs, sweeping the floor, hanging a shelf, or tightening a screw.

Look around and see what little things you can do to make a big difference. Just taking that bag of old toys to the charity store or recycling that stack of newspapers can improve the look of your garage.

Small Changes, Big Results

A few simple projects yield big results. Is the garage looking dull and dirty? Put a fresh coat of paint on the walls. Are the steps into the house cluttered with shoes and boots? Move them to a shelf or shoe rack or other place that you designate as the spot for shoes and boots.

This clever shoe rack in the garage keeps the area looking neat and prevents tripping over loose shoes.

Photo by Schulte

A pegboard is a simple solution for organizing tools.

Photo by Bunjipeg

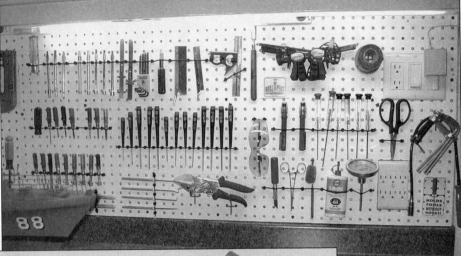

The toolbox is a ready-made storage system designed for tool storage.

Photo by Robert Russell

Do you spend lots of time looking for your tools?

Think of an organizing system and arrange your tools by function, frequency of use, or in alphabetical order. We discuss how in Chapters 12 and 13.

Hang It

Look at all the unused wall space in the garage. Get that stuff off the floor.

Your hanging system can be as simple as a nail pounded into the wall or as fancy as installing a complete wall system with spots for hanging everything. Pulleys are popular options for lifting heavier things off the floor. Your choices really are limited only by your imagination.

$ Loose Change _____

Use a *10d nail* driven at a slight upward angle to hang a variety of objects. Be sure that the nail is driven into a wall stud. A bungee cord or a loop of heavy cord attached to what you are hanging makes it possible to hang many different objects.

ABC Definitions _____

Nails are measured by their lengths using either inches or pennies. The penny is designated by the letter "d". The 2d nail measures in at one inch. For each additional "d", you should add $\frac{1}{4}$" to the length. So a 10d nail will be 3" long. The system changes for anything bigger than a 10d nail. This system originated centuries ago and was probably based on the cost of 100 nails.

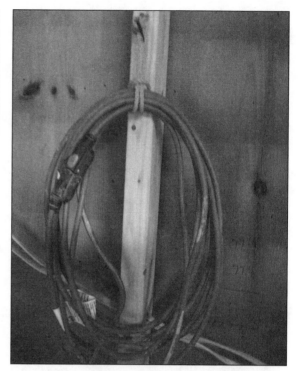

A rope around this extension cord makes it easy to hang on a simple 10d nail.

Photo by Robert Russell

Hooks screwed into the ceiling securely hold bikes and keep them out of the way.

Photo by Robert Russell

Consider the possibility of systems used elsewhere in the house and using that same system in the garage. Would a coat rack be useful for hanging snowsuits or other wet, sports, or seasonal gear?

Drive It Home

A variety of threaded hooks can be used in both wall studs and ceiling joists to hang anything from small tools to bicycles and lawn mowers. Be sure to use sufficiently large hooks that are capable of holding the required weight capacity of whatever you are hanging. Hooks will differ by diameter and thread length. Carefully read the package to find the proper size to safely hold whatever you wish to hang. Make sure that you have properly drilled a pilot hole into a suitable stud or rafter before screwing in the hook. Quality hooks provide complete instructions for installation.

This keeps the ladder out of the way.

Photo by Hyloft

Shelf It

The options for shelving are many:

- Wired
- Wood
- Metal
- Plastic
- One piece
- Bookcase
- Cabinet

You can locate the shelving above the windows or doors, or in the rafters. Shelves may be installed on a wall or they may be freestanding units. Use your imagination and you will find all sorts of places for shelves.

When space is tight, look above the doors or windows for a place to put shelves.

Photo by Hyloft

Don't let that empty space on the wall go to waste.

Photo by Hyloft

Drive It Home

For quick, easy, and cheap tool organization, buy several inexpensive toolboxes (less that $10 each). Label them for plumbing, electrical, car, carving, or whatever else you have and fill them with the corresponding tools and hardware.

A single shelf is a simple way to keep things off the floor.

Photo by Mary Mihaly

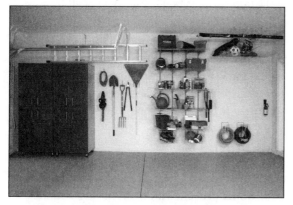

This system is perfect for storing many items.

Photo by ClosetMaid

Shelves bear a lot of weight when loaded, so it is necessary to figure what the safe limits are for the shelves that you use. Manufactured shelving, whether freestanding or using wall-mounted brackets, will clearly specify load limits. If you wish to construct your own shelving, consult a knowledgeable person at a lumberyard. They should be able to recommend whether to use boards, plywood, or composite shelving for your project. Shelves are practical for keeping things out of the reach of small children and adding high-up storage that might not be possible at lower levels because of clearance issues.

Stack It and Store It

Sometimes you need a storage system that is quickly and easily expandable and just as easy to rearrange. Molded plastic shelving units sold at the big-box home improvement centers can be stacked and expanded as needed. Another option to consider is the plastic storage bins that come in a variety of sizes and colors. They can be stacked and moved around as needed. A disadvantage to carefully consider is that the entire stack of bins must be moved if you need something in the bottom container. Plan accordingly.

Warning Light

Watch load limits. Place heavy items on the bottom and lighter items on the top.

Be sure to label your storage containers carefully so you can see and easily read the label facing you. If you put the label on the lid or don't use a label at all, you will have to unstack everything and open it just to find whatever you are looking for. This is a waste of time.

You can stack or collapse the shelves and the bins into much smaller spaces when they are not in use. They usually can be nested together.

Smaller containers help sort things.

Photo by Jared Newman

Complete Storage Systems

The number and variety of storage systems has increased dramatically in recent years with the growing garage market. Garage organization is becoming one of the top home remodeling projects. This is right up there with remodeling kitchens and bathrooms. New houses are being built with elaborate systems already installed. When you begin considering these systems, don't limit yourself to just one usage. Think outside of the storage box and be creative. Look over the following illustrated systems and think about how they might work for you. We will explore these and other systems in detail in Chapter 13.

Multiuse Possibilities

You might have some extra space in your garage, but not quite what you would need for two distinct areas. There could be several ways to get around this issue. The most obvious is to make your garage space a multipurpose area. Maybe you need some closed storage with built-in shelves. You might consider using the door as a place for hanging tools or gardening equipment. Would you like a place to work on a hobby? Think about arranging that area to multitask. Maybe some days it will be your

potting area, while other days it must function as a woodworking shop. Look for ways to arrange things so that they can be easily moved or hidden away. Maybe a work area slides out from underneath a table, but gets hidden away when the car is in the garage. Don't think that you will need two separate areas for a home office and a workbench. There are clever ways to combine the two into one space. There are solutions for any situation.

Home Office

Don't let the lack of space in the interior of your home prevent you from having a home office. Look to the space in your garage. You might need to make some modifications like adding some type of temperature control so you neither freeze in the winter nor swelter in the heat of summer. Extra outlets for the computer and other equipment might also be necessary.

Loose Change

You can make a simple desk for less than $100. Find two 2-drawer file cabinets and lay a hollow core door slab across them. Voilà.

Obviously this garage office has been very successful.

Photo by The Accessories Group

The Koalas practice in a garage in the San Diego area.

Photo by Andrew Hudson

If you are lucky enough to have a lot of extra space in your garage, this is a great place to think about putting a home office. We will go into greater detail in Chapter 14.

Studio

Are you an artist or craftsperson who needs a place where you don't really care about spilling paint on the floor or getting things dirty? Maybe you have a *garage band*.

Definitions

A group of amateur musicians who use the garage as their practice place is called a **garage band**. They may or may not perform garage rock.

Is it a good place to practice or store your instruments? Are you on the driveway to fame? Have you considered if you can do this seasonally or year-round? We'll develop the possibilities more in Chapter 14 and address any mechanical needs such as electricity for amps, a kiln, running water, heat, or additional ventilation.

The Smithy power tool system saves space.

Photo by Smithy

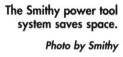

This workshop is perfect for the auto mechanic.

Photo by Sauder

Workshop

Many people work out of their homes or have a business or hobby outside of work. Working on cars or bikes or doing handyman tasks are just a few jobs that might benefit from a dedicated workshop. Maybe you build musical instruments and need a variety of tools. Perhaps you fix old window frames or do woodworking. If your jobs require tools, ventilation, or other special needs, you might enjoy the benefits of having a workshop set up in your garage.

Drive It Home

If you are limited on space, consider one of the multiuse tools like the Shopsmith. Alternatively, you can install caster sets on your stationary tools so that they can be easily moved out of the way.

No more worries about digging out all your supplies and setting them up. This definitely saves time and energy, but requires a decent amount of free space in the garage. If you don't have the space, you can always compromise. A mini-workshop that might need some setting up and tearing down could be the perfect solution. Maybe you could have everything you need fit into a closet. When you need it, you open the doors to the space where your tools are stored. You roll out or fold down your worktable. Maybe a stool you sit on opens up to reveal the materials you need to work with. You've heard it enough already, but you really need to take advantage of all the space you have. The less space you have to work with, the more clever and flexible you need to be.

The Least You Need to Know

◆ An organized garage is a safe garage.

◆ Even simple changes can have big results.

◆ There are many ways to get your stuff off the floor.

◆ One area of the garage can function in many ways.

In This Chapter

- ◆ Assessing and prioritizing your needs
- ◆ Thinking outside the box
- ◆ Taking accurate measurements
- ◆ Drawing a sketch of your garage

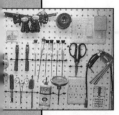  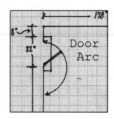   

Chapter 3

Develop the Master Plan

As you realize by now, the options for your garage are many. Now your task is to find out which choices will work best for you. You must take several things into account when deciding how to use your garage in the most efficient way. Assessing your needs will help you focus on some clear-cut goals. What do you need to consider when deciding how to use your garage in the best way possible? Keep reading.

This chapter considers the issues involved in planning a strategy for using your space effectively. Whether your plans include simple solutions or something more extreme, you still need to know your needs.

Some Tough Questions

Some of the considerations that follow might seem obvious; others might seem strange. Keep in mind that your personal priorities, not the Joneses', are of utmost importance. Answer the questions honestly. Answering these questions may raise further questions to consider when evaluating your needs. Make note of them. Also be sure that everyone who uses garage space is involved in this process. Some of the answers to the questions might indicate deeper issues than just the need to put the garage to its best use. Resolving such issues before continuing to the next step will eliminate future conflicts.

This is definitely not an efficient use of the garage.

Photo by Erik Russell

Drive It Home

Be sure to include everybody who uses the garage in this exercise. Having input from just one user sabotages the plan from the start. Achieving success depends on fulfilling the needs of all involved.

Here is a list of questions to get you started:

Purpose

◆ Who will be using the garage?

◆ Is the garage the domain of one person or will the entire family use the space?

◆ Who will decide how the garage will be used?

◆ Is the garage a dumping ground for junk?

◆ Whose stuff is in the garage?

◆ Do you have hobbies that require space?

◆ What belongs in the garage?

◆ Are you willing to park your car out in the elements?

◆ Where do you get out of the car?

◆ Do you need dedicated electric?

◆ Do you need running water in the garage?

◆ Which products are available to make your life easier?

Motivation

◆ Why are you doing this in the first place?

◆ What would you like to accomplish by rethinking its use?

◆ What problems do you see with the garage as it is now?

◆ How would changes impact you?

◆ How will you live during the process?

◆ Do you need to control the temperature in the garage?

◆ Do you want to make additions?

◆ When will you start and complete your project?

◆ Who is going to do the work?

Condition

◆ Is your garage a fire hazard?

◆ Is the garage attached or detached?

◆ Do you have a carport?

◆ Do you have a one-, two-, or three-car garage?

◆ How much space do you have in the garage?

◆ Is there usable exterior space?

◆ Is the garage structurally sound?

◆ Is your garage space awkward?

◆ Does the roof leak?

◆ Are there broken windows?

◆ Do the doors close properly?

◆ Do the doors lock properly?

◆ Is there a garage door opener?

◆ Does the garage door opener work properly?

◆ Does the garage flood?

◆ Does the garage have rodent or insect infestation?

◆ Does your neighborhood allow you to park your car in the driveway?

◆ Does the season affect your use of the garage?

◆ Is there an attic or space above the rafters?

◆ Are there *mechanicals* in the garage?

◆ Is the garage well lit?

◆ Is the floor in good condition?

◆ Are the walls finished?

◆ Do you have adequate electrical outlets?

Definitions

Mechanicals are the physical systems that distribute:

Water. Water heater, water softener, supply lines, drain line, and laundry hookups.

Electrical. Wiring outside of walls, conduit, service panels, lights, switches, and receptacles.

HVAC (heating, ventilation, air conditioning). Furnace, ductwork, humidifier/dehumidifier.

Obviously, all of these questions won't apply to every situation, but answer them as honestly as you can. The more honest and specific you are, the easier and less painful it will be to develop your ideal garage plan. For example, if one person wants to use the garage for parking cars, another wants it to set up a workshop or crafts center, and the kids want it for playing darts, it may be possible to make it a multi-purpose room that suits everybody's needs. On the other hand, one person's unwillingness to compromise or think of alternate solutions may make any attempt at improving the situation impossible.

The preceding questions should make you think about what the perfect garage would be for you. However, what is perfect and what is realistic are two different issues.

A clutter-free garage makes finding things easy.

Photo by Schulte

Say that you have a detached garage and really want a light there. Although this is an ideal situation, it may be unrealistic because of the costs of running electric there. Don't jump to conclusions when determining what is most important to you. There are solutions to the lighting problem that don't involve a major investment of money. Write down what's important. Putting your ideas on paper will help you get organized and help you figure out which projects are needed and realistic and which ones are desires and possibly unrealistic. You need to get to the basics first and think of your needs before satisfying your desires.

Making a List

From your answers to the preceding questions, you now create a needs list with a justification for these needs.

In addition, go and look at your garage. Maybe you don't remember how sloped the roof is or whether there is space above. Check out the *return walls.* Maybe you thought that there was more space there. Your memory of your garage may be faulty, so visit it in person. Take photos if necessary.

Definitions

The **return wall** is the wall that shares the garage door opening.

The return is the distance between the perpendicular side wall of the garage and the opening.

Evaluate Your Needs

Need	Reason
Sink	Not allowed to clean fish in the house
Outlets	Tired of using extension cord for vacuuming the car
Recycling bin	It's in the way in the kitchen
Parking space	Hate scraping snow and ice off the car
Heater	Work on hobbies year-round
Flooring	The dirt floor must go
Floor the attic	Clear the floor space
High cabinets	Store poisons
Plastic containers	Garage is damp
Place to secure garden tools	They fall down, getting in the way of the car
Shelves	Store camping equipment
Tool holders	Tools heaped on the bench

Well, you get the idea. It's your space, your car, and your things, so only you can decide what will work best for you.

Tossing anything onto the bench defeats its purpose.

Photo by Erik Russell

Prioritizing Your Needs

Now that you have completed your needs list, take a hard look at the importance of the needs. You also need to distinguish your needs from your desires. Consider the safety, convenience, and practicality of the items you listed. Keeping hazardous materials stored safely and out of the reach of children and pets should be more important than having a new cover for your car. You also need to consider your budget, as discussed later in this chapter.

Go back to the list you just completed. Give each need a ranking of importance ranging from low to high.

Drive It Home

Do not buy any storage systems or containers at this point. You have a few more steps to work through before you get to that point. On the other hand, having a particular system or certain ideas in mind is perfectly acceptable.

Be sure to compare your notes with others who have been involved in this exercise. Discuss any differences in ratings.

First and Foremost, the Car

Returning from the grocery store, you pause in your driveway, open the garage door, and drive your car into the garage. You step out of the car, remove the groceries, and head into your home.

Squirrels made a nest in this ungaraged car.

Photo by Erik Russell

First and foremost, you are utilizing your garage for what it is meant to be—a place to store the car. Second, you are using the garage as one of the primary entrances and exits from your home. You need to be able to easily place your car or cars in the garage with a simple, straight drive-in maneuver. There should be little chance of damage to the car, to anything in the garage, or to the garage itself. When you exit the car, you should be able to fully open any of the doors, the trunk or hatch, or the hood. You should be able to walk comfortably around the car. In addition, you should be able to safely and easily walk into your home along an unobstructed path.

It was easier for this owner to buy a new car than to dig this one out of the garage.

Photo by Erik Russell

Because the first step in this whole process was to clear out your garage, you should have a clear area where you park your car or where you plan to park the car. We now can proceed to establish the parking space and its boundaries. Driving through the garage door with equal distance from each of the doorjambs, place the car inside the garage so that the rear bumper is about 3 feet from where the garage door will be when closed.

Using masking tape or sidewalk chalk, mark an outline of your car on the garage floor. Now open all the doors and the rear hatch if you have one. Mark an outline of each of these on the floor. Close the doors. Now make two more outlines around the original car outline. The first will be 2 feet away from the original outline and the second 3 feet away. These designate the minimum and the adequate clearances needed to comfortably move around the car.

Typical Car Sizes

Model	Length	Width
2-Door Coupes	(inches)	(inches)
Mini Cooper S	143.9	66.5
Volkswagen New Beetle	161.1	67.9
4-Door Sedans	(inches)	(inches)
Ford Taurus SEL	197.7	73.0
Honda Civic LX	174.6	67.5
Toyota Camry	189.2	70.7
Volvo V70 Wagon	185.4	71.0
SUVs, Pickups, and Vans	(inches)	(inches)
Chevrolet Tahoe	196.9	78.9
Ford Excursion	226.7	79.9
Lexus LX470	192.5	76.4
Lincoln Navigator	204.8	79.8
Dodge Dakota	218.8	71.7
Dodge Grand Caravan	200.5	78.6

Warning Light

The doors of a two-door car are usually longer than the doors of a four-door car. Don't assume that the arc of doors from different cars will be the same. Unless you will always park one car in the same place, consider the measurements of all cars that will be parked in the garage.

This is how it is supposed to work. What if your garage is not cooperating? Car dimensions vary, and garage dimensions are not always necessarily sufficient to allow for these clearances. Prioritize your needs and then compromise and adjust the clearances. You need to comfortably get in and out of the driver's seat. Do you have a young child with a child seat? If so, allow maximum clearance for removing and replacing the child seat and for helping your child in and out of the car. Where is the path from each of the car doors, especially the driver's, to the entrance of your home? Do you need frequent access to the trunk? You may have support columns or other structural or mechanical invasions into the idealized parking space that need to be addressed. When you have established a tentative placement of the car in the garage, you can move on to taking accurate measurements of the entire interior space.

This car is truly the king of this garage.

Photo by The Accessories Group

Think Outside the Box

Thinking outside the box is important when it comes to your garage solutions, especially when working with limited space. Take an inventory of what has to stay in the garage and what will be moved into the garage.

Drive It Home

Think beyond the obvious when considering storage solutions. Look up for storage possibilities, such as pulley systems that store bicycles at the ceiling or upright pole systems that store two bicycles vertically.

If your tools are heaped in a pile on a bench, perhaps a simple toolbox or a pegboard will solve that problem.

Before you start thinking about what will go into the garage, be sure the rest of the house is cleaned first. Because the garage is the catchall, the first place that those leftovers from the rest of the house will go is into the garage.

What Needs to Be Improved?

Perhaps your garage is already neat and clean. What could you do to make it more efficient? Maybe all your tools are hanging on a pegboard in random order.

You could organize them by the amount of use the tools get or by the type of tool. Is the hammer next to a wrench or next to other hammers? Perhaps labeling boxes in the garage would save you time. Tired of looking at that half-finished woodworking project that you started years ago? Put it into a better spot or throw it away. Make a list of things that would improve your garage.

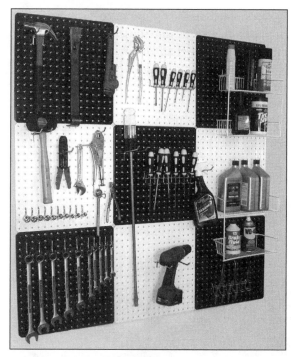

Pegboard is simple and easy to install and neatly organizes tools.

Photo by Alligator Board

Storage, Storage, and More Storage

"Off the floor, onto the wall, and out of the driveway" is the motto of garage storage suppliers. Look up to the ceiling and onto the walls. In an unfinished garage, there is empty space between the studs on the walls and the rafters above. There are simple and more elaborate ways to use this (and any other space for that matter).

Solutions need not be expensive, difficult to install, or have lots of pieces. The wide variety of products on the market means you will find something perfect for your space. Whether you need just a few hooks, a pegboard, or want a proprietary system, you can find something out there to suit your needs.

Don't exclude the option of recycling other things from around the house. Maybe you just remodeled the kitchen and have old cabinets that would prove useful in the garage. Have you replaced some wall shelves? Do you have old milk bottles, baby food jars, or soup cans? There are endless possibilities for reusing other containers for storage options.

List the types of things you need to store in the garage.

You will appreciate having a dedicated spot for your gardening duties.

Photo by ClosetMaid

The storage possibilities themselves might be overwhelming and might cause some real excitement. Under no circumstances should you go out and start buying storage products. That will come later, so please, please be patient.

Take Accurate Measurements

You may have architectural drawings of your house that include the garage and think that those are adequate for your plan. However, what appears on paper may not be the reality. Adjustments in construction or revisions after the drawings were done, settling in an older home, or modifications made at a later date can affect the interior dimensions of your garage.

Drive It Home

Take multiple measurements for dimensions such as ceiling height. Use the smallest measurement when planning your space. It is much easier to leave a slight gap than to try to force something into a too-small space.

Taking accurate measurements is one of the most important steps in creating a successful organization of your garage. Follow these suggestions to get your plan off to a successful start:

- Collect your measuring tools, some pencils and paper, and an assistant to help taking measurements over long distances.
- Take your time and take each measurement twice.
- Accurately record each measurement.
- Round each measurement to the nearest eighth of an inch.

Measuring Tools

Your basic measuring tool is the tape measure, which comes in a variety of lengths and widths. For measuring long distances, you want a tape that is at least 25 feet long. Do not use one that is less than three quarters of an inch wide. Smaller widths cannot be extended and remain rigid for lengths of more than 6 feet.

Warning Light

The metal hook on the end of the measuring tape slides slightly to measure both inside and outside dimensions. As the tape ages, inaccuracies come from use and abuse. Check its accuracy by comparing to a ruler. Alternatively, start your measurements at the 1-inch mark. Just remember to subtract an inch from your final measurement.

A steel rule or wooden yardstick is also helpful for measuring smaller dimensions. It becomes tedious to use it repeatedly over long distances, and you run the risk of compounding any small errors into much larger ones.

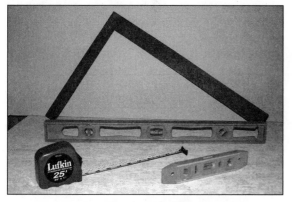

A square, large level, torpedo level, and tape measure.

Photo by Theresa Russell

When using a tape measure, it often proves helpful to have an assistant holding the "dumb" end of the tape while you read the "smart" end. There are a variety of sonic and laser devices to make this a one-person operation. This can be a pricey option if you are not going to use the device again.

A framing square is handy for determining whether walls, floor, and ceiling are perpendicular to each other, but not necessarily vertical.

A level proves useful for determining whether walls are truly vertical and whether there is a slope in the garage floor. Levels come in a variety of shapes and sizes. A 48" level is ideal for checking your walls and floor. The smaller torpedo level is useful for fitting into confined spaces and for installing shelving and cabinets later on.

Measure It

First, roughly sketch a *floor plan*, an *elevation plan* for each of the four walls, and a *ceiling plan*. I like to use six large sheets (14"×17") of blank paper for my sketches. I record all measurements and notes, and then transfer these to graph paper for more elegant and accurate drawings.

Definitions

The **floor plan** is the horizontal view of your space. Think about what you would see if you were looking down from the ceiling.

The **wall elevation** is the vertical view of your space. Think about what you would see if you were standing in front of the walls.

The **ceiling plan** is what you would see if you were lying on the floor looking up.

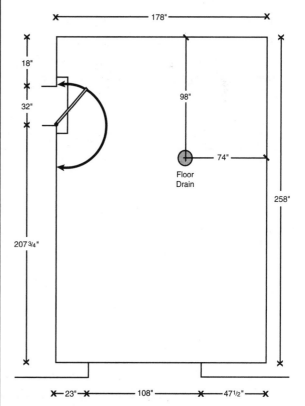

Start the measuring process with a rough drawing of the floor.

Photo by Robert Russell

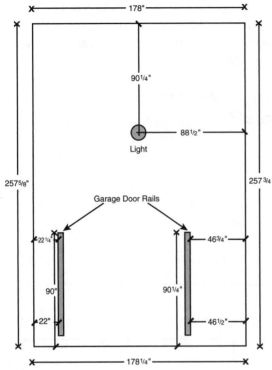

Don't forget to measure the ceiling and mark any protrusions.

Photo by Robert Russell

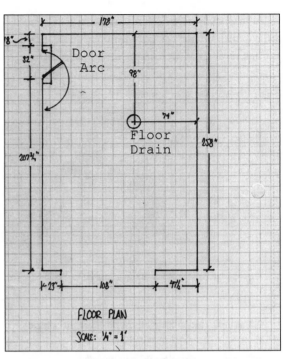

When you have your rough drawing, transfer it to graph paper using the scale of your choice, although $\frac{1}{4}$" to 1' is simplest.

Photo by Robert Russell

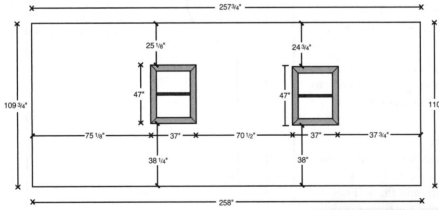

Be sure to include windows, doors, and anything that interferes with the line of the wall.

Photo by Robert Russell

Measuring twice is important for accuracy and will save time and money in the long run.

Photo by Theresa Russell

Start at the top and measure the length and width of the ceiling. This is where your assistant becomes especially helpful, along with a couple of ladders. Sketch any lights, garage door brackets and rails, and electrical and mechanical fixtures mounted on the ceiling on your drawing and locate them by indicating the distances from two perpendicular walls. If you have open rafters, measure the distance between them. If you have pull-down stairs to an attic, measure the outside perimeter and include it on your drawing.

Drive It Home

You can measure long distances by yourself without a sonic or laser device fairly easily by dividing the distance into two smaller parts and adding the resulting measurements. This technique works well for measuring ceiling height. Make a mark at a convenient location, measuring the distance from the floor to your mark and from the ceiling to your mark. Add the two numbers together.

Next pick a corner and measure the walls going around the garage in one direction until you return to the starting corner. You need three horizontal measurements: at the floor, at the ceiling (which you just measured), and halfway between the floor and ceiling. Take several vertical measurements, recording each in its relative position on your sketch. Locate any windows, doors, electrical outlets, or other structural or mechanical features on your sketch.

After you have finished with all four walls, record the horizontal wall measurements at the floor level onto your floor plan. Open any door that opens into the garage and sketch the arc it makes over its entire travel. Locate the footprint or outline of the pull-down stairs on the floor. Locate any other features, such as drains or bases of support columns. Finally, locate the car outline you constructed earlier to complete your floor plan.

Formulate Your Budget

The variety of options and costs available today are a huge help as you stick to a budget. You may make simple changes that involve more sweat than dollars. And if you do use organizing systems, you can spend as little or as much as you want and still have a successful outcome.

Sit down and think about how much you want to spend. There is a solution for every budget. Be sure to consider any labor costs when figuring your budget. If you are considering major changes such as flooring the attic, replacing the garage door, or upgrading the electricity, include labor costs in your budget. Even if you are making simple changes, but don't know how to proceed, you need to call in an expert and pay accordingly.

Keep in mind that all experts are not just construction related. The professional organizer, junk hauler, or eBay specialist also charges fees.

The Least You Need to Know

◆ Before you start your project, have a written plan.

◆ Prioritize your needs and customize your plan accordingly.

◆ Keep an open mind and think outside the box.

◆ Thoroughness now will save later costs, frustrations, and time.

◆ Know your budget and remember to include labor costs.

In This Chapter

◆ Determining the sequence of events

◆ Setting a date

◆ Organizing time, help and equipment

◆ Minimizing inconvenience and stress

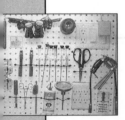

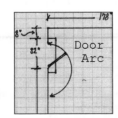

Chapter 4

Get Ready, Get Set

Finally! We are down to the last few details you need to consider before committing time, energy, and money to your garage solutions project. Like any project, the details could cause certain inconveniences, even if it is as simple as not being able to park your car in the garage. This can be a real problem in a neighborhood that doesn't allow street parking. Or perhaps you can't park cars in a driveway. How long will things be in an uproar? Do you have the time to commit to the project? Might it be better to wait before starting? Projects take tools, and it will be necessary to assemble all the tools and supplies you need before you start your project. You don't want to waste precious time running back and forth to the store to buy cleaning supplies, paint, or a screwdriver when you are in the middle of the project. While you are hanging a shelf is not the best time to realize that a drill would be handy or that you need an extension cord.

If you have issues that could slow the process down, you might need to call on help. If so, be ready when they show up. Volunteers don't want to stand around waiting for something to do. If you hired help, delays will cost you wasted dollars. Scheduling is very important.

You Need Some Order

Let's get our ducks in a row. First, find a day, week, or month that will allow you to give your undivided attention to beginning your garage solution. Depending on where you live, the weather may be a big factor. Do you have vacation time coming up? Do your kids have school vacations coming up soon? That can be a plus or a minus. Second, will your help be available? If so, get a commitment. Third, gather your equipment. Have your cleaning supplies ready and any repair equipment, such as ladders, available. Finally, get to work and get the job done.

Drive It Home _____

Often, getting started is the hardest part of an organizing project. A professional organizer can help you create a plan to complete your projects by creating a vision for success, deciding the resources you need, creating a timeline, and breaking the project down into small and manageable pieces that can be tackled over time.

Daily Planner

This is a job and should be treated as such. You are acting as the contractor on this project and need to come up with a reasonable schedule. The pest inspector can't do much if the garage is full of stuff. The painters will have a difficult time painting if there is still a pile of junk against the wall. The leak in the garage needs to be repaired before stuff is returned to the garage.

Set a Date

You have decided the best time to start your project, and that is well and good. But now you need to make a commitment and write it down on the calendar. No rescheduling because somebody has great seats to a concert or the game! This project is important. If you write it down, you are more likely to consider it important.

Drive It Home _____

Get out your calendar and write down the date that you plan to start your project. Having this in writing gives importance to your project, acts as an external motivator, and makes you commit to it.

It won't be easy to give up other activities that you love, but you have to just get it done as scheduled. You have already found a place to store your stuff, and you have found friends and family to help you clear out your space. Even if your project will only take a few hours, you need to dedicate yourself to those few hours. The hours you spend now will save you many hours later. Won't it be nice to go to the exact same place in the garage each time you need your torx screwdriver? Won't it be nice to know that you won't have to sort through unmarked boxes of stuff to find the holiday decorations? Use an online calendar, your home calendar, and the PDA calendar to save the date. Make it a fun activity. Treat yourself to something special when the project is finished. Reward yourself with the cordless tool that you have been dreaming of or with a new potting bench for your gardening needs.

Find Help If Necessary

You have your date, but can you do all the work yourself? Do you know somebody who is a great organizer or who has a label maker and loves to make labels? Maybe you need someone who can tell you the names of all those tools you inherited from Grandpa.

If you have physical issues, you may need help lifting, reaching, or bending down. Now is the time to think about the help you might need. Can you hire a neighborhood kid to get the stuff down from the attic or move boxes?

Do you need somebody with a pickup truck, van, or a large truck to haul your stuff away?

If you plan to paint or powerwash or use tools that you don't own or don't know how to use, find help. Do you have something really heavy stored in the garage that you can't lift? Do you need a car with a hitch to move that restoration project out of the garage?

Warning Light _____

Poor lifting techniques can cause injury and pain. Remember to use good body mechanics when lifting and moving objects in your garage. Engage your core, bend your knees, and use your leg muscles to lift. Heavy objects that are located at or above waist level should not be lifted with your feet on the floor, since you are engaging only your back muscles, rather than your thigh muscles.

Snacks and Beverages

You don't want to delay the project because you forgot to have food and refreshments around for you and your helpers. Make sure to have plenty of water and snacks available during the time you are working and plan on meals for the time your helpers are at your home.

Gather Materials

You don't want to waste the time that you have set aside to work on your garage running back and forth to find the proper equipment for the job. This is a list of tools to get started.

Safety

Safety comes first. Keep it a priority. Some very involved projects might require more safety gear.

Some basic things that you and your helpers need include eye protection, dust masks, and work gloves.

Clearing, Moving, and Sorting

Whether you need help or not, you want to have some equipment handy that makes things easier to move. For those with weak backs or other physical issues, having an able-bodied helper will do the trick. For moving heavy things, take advantage of a hand truck or dolly.

Loose Change _____

If you don't have the equipment to help you move things, consider buying it from a discount tool warehouse. Things such as dollies, hand trucks, and tarps are often inexpensive and may be cheaper than renting them.

Use moving pads to protect those antiques. A tarp makes a good surface for moving lots of stuff in one big yank. It is also good to use for sorting the things that you are removing from the garage. There is no one best way to sort that works for every situation. The three-pile technique—keep, toss, and recycle—will work well as a default technique, if you need one. Other things you need to have are markers, labels, tape, and containers.

Surface Cleaning

When you get everything moved out of the garage, sweep it, dust it, and wash the windows. Have a broom and dustpan or Shop Vac and garbage bags handy.

Repairs and Installation

Separate the tools you will need for projects that need repair and for the things you are installing. Put them in a place where they are easily accessible.

Anticipate Inconvenience

What project have you done that didn't cause some inconvenience? Perhaps you can't use the garage. Maybe you have to move some stuff into the house. Or maybe you can't walk on the newly painted floor for a while. There is always inconvenience. The trick is to be proactive and try to reduce the inconvenience as much as possible. Plan on it and work around it. Following are some issues to consider before starting your garage project.

Length of Time

Time and money will be your biggest investments in this project. The length of time is a factor in when to start the project and when to do certain parts of the project. Suppose your project of painting the garage floor will take several days, the forecast is for rain, and you need to move everything out of the garage. You either have to change your start date or have an alternative place to store the contents of the garage.

> **Warning Light** _____
>
> Don't think that organizing is a one-time deal. The initial organization will require some time and effort. But if you don't get into the mind-set of staying organized, you may be wasting your time and money starting this project in the first place.

Your free time is also a major consideration. If you start a project when you know you will be working overtime or have a major deadline to meet, you are just setting yourself up for stress. However, if you are the type who thrives under pressure, this may not bother you at all. What if you work out of your garage or use the garage to do certain things that are job- or hobby-related? How long can you survive without having access to your table saw or air compressor? Can you move it somewhere in the interim? Can you divide your space in half and do half at a time? Think about what works for you.

Unavailability of Tools

This works on both ends. If you need to rent something (for example, a powerwasher to clean your floor) and it is already reserved for the dates that you want to use it or if you are borrowing it from a friend who won't have it available, you need to think again about your dates or the order in which you will attack your project.

> **$ Loose Change** _____
>
> Keep a collection of inexpensive tools such as hammers, screwdrivers, pliers, and wrenches in a small toolbox or bag that you store in the trunk of your car. This way you don't need to worry about not having access to basic tools that may be temporarily inaccessible.

What if you need a ladder to patch a leak in the roof and it is stored elsewhere? Emergency repairs go hand-in-hand with homeownership. Keep tools like screwdrivers and wrenches in an easily accessible place for the duration of your project.

Move the Car

This sounds like an easy feat, but what if the car you need to move won't start or is a project car? Some housing associations don't allow cars to be parked in the driveway or on the street.

You need to decide what your options are and figure out what you will do if your car isn't convenient to you. That is why you plan everything in advance. Maybe moving the car means donating it to charity or having the junkyard come and get it out.

Unexpected Issues

Even the best-laid plans have glitches. Somebody hit a power pole and the electricity is out for hours. Your neighbor called nuisance abatement when you moved that old wooden boat that has been in the garage for years waiting for restoration. You parked it in the driveway and covered it with a tarp. You caught a cold or got called in for mandatory overtime at work. It has rained for days with no sign of stopping. What can you do? You could have a plan B formulated, which might entail moving your start date. Or you might be able to call on friends and family. Maybe you could rent a generator if the electric has gone out. The weather could be a problem, and you might even find some major work that needs to be done and the experts are booked for months. Flexibility is key; and no matter how devastating the setbacks are to your project, you need to sit back, relax, and take it in stride (as frustrating as it can be). This may send you back to square one of the planning process, but this time you will be an expert at it.

The Least You Need to Know

- Carefully plan the sequence of events to complete your task in a timely manner.
- Commit yourself and your resources to getting the job done.
- Don't hesitate to ask for help in completing the job.
- Gather all the materials and equipment you need before starting your project.

In This Chapter

- ◆ Make a commitment
- ◆ Evaluate your skills
- ◆ Decide, delegate, or contract
- ◆ Know which experts you need
- ◆ Find a qualified expert

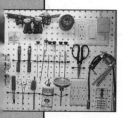

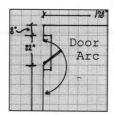

Chapter 5

Expert Help

Big plans call for many hours of work. You can't just hope that what you want to accomplish happens overnight when the garage fairy waves his magic wand. You might not have the time, motivation, or skills to work on your project. That is when you call in the experts. Experts don't have to be people who do this type of work for a living. Maybe your sister can paint like no other. Perhaps your neighbor is an expert at installing garage doors. Or your mother is a great organizer.

Your mission in this chapter is to decide who will be doing the work. You may be comfortable with some jobs but might want experts to do the plumbing, electric, or heating. You may be qualified to do everything that needs to be done. However, if you don't have the time to do it, experts will help you complete the project in a timely manner.

If you have no clue where to start, a garage organizer may be the perfect place to start. They know how to guide you through overwhelming projects. They can motivate you and help with a design, strategy, and tips for improving your garage space. If you have a leaky roof or an insect infestation, get some help. Make sure that all of this is included in your plan. *Most importantly, for this project to be successful you must commit to it and take it seriously.*

Labor Pains

Where should you begin? What can you do to prepare for this job? First you need to analyze your skills and your time. What are you able to do? Can you do it quickly and with professional-looking results? If you hire people to perform any work in your garage, you can expect that about just more than half of the cost will go toward labor. On the other hand, if you buy a complete storage system, installation may be included with the purchase.

Warning Light _____

Do not rely on just a license or fancy ad when choosing an expert. Ask the expert for references from past customers. The competent expert will gladly let you talk with people who were happy with the work.

Your Skills or Lack Thereof

You need to take a serious inventory of your skills and plan accordingly. If you are easily distracted and can't stand tedious jobs, think carefully about assigning yourself jobs that aren't stimulating enough for you. Maybe somebody else loves to sort through things or is a great organizer or motivator. Maybe you hate working alone and accomplish much more with another person working side by side with you. When you think about your skills, don't necessarily think of concrete skills such as being good with a hammer or table saw. More implicit skills such as organizing or visualizing are necessary components of any project.

Checklist of Skills

Sit down with pen and paper and list your skills that are pertinent to your project. Include both concrete and intangible skills. Think about what you do well. If you can gather a crowd to complete a task, write that down. Some people can envision the outcome of any project. Are you one of them? Cleaning is a task that some love and others despise. Write this down. Write down more-concrete skills such as painting, carpentry, hanging and finishing drywall, or whatever other skills you can think of. Now add to your list all the necessary tasks you either don't like doing or those you have no experience doing. This should provide a fairly complete list of tasks to get you going. Add any more that come to mind as you think about your project.

Next to your list draw three columns and label them Able, Willing, and Time. Go down the Able column and put a check mark next to those tasks that you have the skills to accomplish. Then go down the Willing column and put a check mark next to those tasks that you are willing to do. Finally, go down the Time column and put a check mark next to those tasks that you have time to do. Be honest. Even though you might be completely qualified to do every task, you might realize that you don't have the time or the motivation to do it for this project.

A Sample of a Jobs List

Jobs	Are you able?	Are you willing?	Do you have the time?
Heavy lifting			
Cleaning			
Painting			
Organizing			
Electrical work			
Hanging shelves			
Rubbish disposal			

This should give you an informative list of tasks that you can now delegate or hire out to others if necessary.

Who Ya Gonna Call?

A review of your list shows that although you can paint, you don't have time to do it (because you need to complete your project in a timely manner). You want to add some electrical circuits, but you can barely change a light bulb.

Don't despair. There is help for the smallest to largest task. Your job now is to call in the help. Coordinating these experts to arrive and do their jobs is a skill in itself.

Professional Organizer

This is a growing profession of people in high demand. Everybody can use somebody to help them organize. A *professional organizer* usually comes into your house and asks questions to assess your needs. Your needs may be simple and require just minor changes or a simple organizing system. On the other hand, you may need lots of help coming up with a plan or even getting a jump-start. A good organizer can help you from the beginning of your project to the end.

Definitions

According to the National Association of Professional Organizers (NAPO), "a **professional organizer** enhances the lives of clients by designing systems and processes using organizing principles and through transferring organizing skills. A professional organizer also educates the public on organizing solutions and the resulting benefits."

Professional organizers deal with situations like yours on a regular basis. Their experience enables them to quickly find solutions to your organizational problems that might not be obvious to you. They can also help you overcome your organizational dilemmas and keep you on track.

You can search in the Yellow Pages for an organizer or go online to find somebody in your area.

Drive It Home

Diane, a professional organizer, says that the biggest problem most people struggle with is deciding to get rid of stuff. A professional organizer can be of invaluable assistance when you find it tough to part with things you own. "I work with my clients by leading them through a series of inquiries to explore just why they find it difficult to get rid of a particular item."

Structural and Mechanical Experts

There are a variety of tradespeople available to solve your skill and time problems. For the exterior components of your garage, you can call a roofer to repair a leak, to add downspouts, or to replace shingles. An electrician can add extra outlets to your garage, bring service to the garage, or update the service in your garage. Rough carpenters build the skeleton of your garage. Maybe you want an extra closet or a floored attic. This is the guy to contact. A finish carpenter can change doors or hinges and add trim to your door or window. If you need to change the location of an exterior door or add a window, call a rough carpenter.

Do you need a new garage door? Call a garage door professional.

If you enjoy a hobby such as pottery, you might benefit from a nearby water source. A plumber can help you get running water into your garage. Your garage may also have an outdoor spigot that needs a better location. The plumber can handle this job. He also could add an additional spigot to solve your gardening needs. The HVAC guy is the expert at controlling the temperature of your house. He can add venting, heating, or air conditioning to your garage.

Drive It Home

As you develop your task list, other special labor needs may become apparent, especially in the early stages of clearing and cleaning. Junk haulers, eBay trading assistants, and professional cleaners are just a few more people who can help you achieve your goals.

Drywall guys and painters, like many of these experts, stick to their own specialty, but you may be able to find a general contractor who can provide an expert for any part of your project.

The foundation specialist can make sure that the foundation of your garage is intact and sufficiently strong to hold up the walls in the garage. He can repair any damage that may have been caused from the ground leveling or from water seeping alongside the foundation.

Loose Change

The cost of labor is about 60 percent of the costs associated with a project. The more you can do yourself, the more money you will save. Just remember, taking on projects you can't complete will cost a lot more in the long run.

The masonry and concrete expert is the person who can repair your garage floor and pour an entirely new floor. She also does work to the structure of your garage, should yours be made of concrete blocks or brick.

If you want to give your garage floor a new look and new covering, the flooring specialist is the expert to call.

Systems Manufacturer

The company that produces some of the interesting products you want to install in your garage may have their own contractors who are trained to install, modify, or repair any of the products that they manufacture. Some also keep lists of people who can help you with their products. They range from the organizer to the general contractors. No matter how much assistance you need, you are sure to find it.

Local Hardware Store

Don't overlook your local hardware or home supply center. Many of the systems manufacturers train their local suppliers in techniques of installing their products and may also have an expert who will show you the best products for your needs. Some of the larger home supply centers even offer classes home improvement. You might want to check with your local supply center to see what they offer that might be of help to you.

Friends and Family

Your friends and family may possess just the skills that you need for your project. Uncle Bill might be an electrician who would love to help you out. (Maybe you have helped him move several times.) Some people love to paint and wouldn't pass up an opportunity to help out. Call in those favors.

Choosing an Expert

If you do need help, find somebody, for example, a *general contractor*, qualified to do the work. One of the best ways to find a suitable person is through word of mouth. Ask your friends and neighbors who they hired. Ask whether they were satisfied with the work. If somebody tells you they were dissatisfied with the work, note who did it and don't call that person. Remember that licensing requirements vary by state and region. If you live in a state that doesn't require licensing for home remodelers, you will have to look at other qualifications to help in your selection.

Definitions

A **general contractor** supervises all aspects of work done at the job site. The general contractor hires and pays the subcontractors, coordinates permits and inspections, and purchases all materials.

Other places to find help include the following:

- Yellow Pages under the appropriate heading. Check out those who are bonded and insured.
- Trade associations keep lists of members.
- Licensing boards have lists of licensed members.
- Building supply stores keep lists of independent contractors.

- Often, contractors put a sign in the yard where they are working. Also look at names on service vehicles.
- Online referral sites have listings by trade.
- Other experts often can recommend qualified people.

There are many experts to choose from. It is up to you to find the expert who is a good match for your project.

If you decide to do the work yourself, make sure that you are a good choice, too. Be sure to subject yourself to the same standards that you would apply to somebody you hire.

The Least You Need to Know

- Decide whether you are qualified to do the work on your project.
- Be honest when evaluating your skills and time constraints.
- Know your limits.
- Choose your experts carefully.
- Ask experts for names of past clients.
- Hire only dependable experts with a good reputation.

In This Part

Part **2**

Call to Action

You've taken the time to analyze your needs, develop your master plan, and line up the help to assist you. You've started thinking about what's going to work best in your garage and how to pay for it. You circled a date on your calendar, and that day has arrived.

Now it's time to put on your work clothes and go out to the garage. It may seem a daunting task to clear it all out and clean it. But don't worry; we help you approach this task in such a way that you will get through it as painlessly as possible. You will experience a tremendous sense of accomplishment when you have finished.

After you stand in your clean garage and admire your feat, take a good close look inside and outside to make sure that everything is okay. Next start thinking in detail about designing your dream garage and making any modifications or repairs you need. Don't feel intimidated by any of these tasks. You can call in any number of experts to do some or all of the required work. Let's clean up and design that space.

In This Chapter

- ◆ Evaluating your organizational needs
- ◆ Sorting through your stuff
- ◆ Getting rid of stuff
- ◆ Disposing of hazardous waste

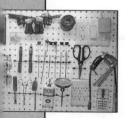

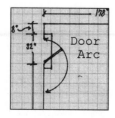

Chapter 6

Pile Drivers

The garage does have the reputation of being the main storage area of many houses. After all, it is a great place for storage. In fact, many newer homes even have extra space for storage, complete with storage units. What is the storage situation like in your garage? Is everything in its place? Or has the situation gotten out of control in your garage? Can you go out there and quickly find the tool that you need? Do you know what is in the boxes stacked along the wall? Do you have several of the same tools because you can't remember where you put them after you use them? If you can honestly say you know where everything is, and that doesn't include knowing exactly where in a heap you can find something, you have been doing a good job. On the other hand, if you can't find things, you have some work ahead of you.

You must clear out your garage before you can start on any project. Fortunately, there are many ways to rid yourself of your excess or unneeded possessions that are taking up all that precious space in your garage. Even if your garage is pretty empty, it is a good idea to get rid of unnecessary items on a regular basis to keep the garage functioning smoothly. Taking a regular inventory of the things in your garage is an excellent way to keep it from turning into a giant storage bin.

Organize Your Piles

Those piles of boxes, tools, toys, and sporting goods may look formidable. Your best plan of action is going to be to sort the things in your garage. If you don't start sorting from the start, you will just have the same problem you are trying to resolve, but in a different area or different configuration. Basically, you need to decide what you want to keep and what you are willing and able get rid off. There will be things you may not be able to get rid of but are not sure whether you should keep, so these will go into their own pile. Try hard to make a decision about everything at the start. The "undecided" pile should be the smallest of the piles you make.

Drive It Home

Our feng shui expert, Mary, says that every item in your space must serve you or nurture you. If you don't use it or love it, it's clutter and it's holding you back. Guilt is *not* a reason to keep things. On a wintry night, Aunt Martha's ugly comforter could be keeping someone warm. It's just stuff, and somebody needs it. Giving makes good karma.

Removing this clutter will free up a lot of space.

Photo by Erik Russell

That's a Keeper

You should know right off the bat certain things that you will be keeping in your garage: a tool chest, bicycles, the snow blower, and gardening tools. Be sure that the things you keep are in good condition and serve a practical purpose. You can start sorting them in a way that has meaning to you.

When you've determined what you want to keep, organize it by type, size, or some other way that suits your needs. So if you have a bunch of sporting equipment, put that all together in one pile. Do the same with tools, lawn and garden, and whatever else. This will help you later when it comes to deciding what you need to do to properly store these in your garage.

Put It Somewhere Else

To successfully complete your garage project, you may need to store things that will remain in your garage somewhere else for a while. Maybe what you want to keep has been waiting to be repaired. Send it out right now and get it fixed. Because the garage often becomes the storage place for everything, some of the things you are keeping may not belong in the garage in the first place. Put them where they really belong. Be sure that the garage is the best place for a particular item. If it really doesn't belong in the garage, move it to its proper place.

Store It Temporarily

Either find another place in the house to keep your things or get a storage unit until you have completed your plans. There are portable storage units that can be delivered and left at your house for temporary storage. These companies can also deliver a unit to you and move it to a remote location after you have filled it up. Just be sure to check whether these big boxes are permitted in your neighborhood.

Maybe you can survive with storing your bicycles in the garden shed for the few days you are concentrating on the garage. Move the recycling bin into the kitchen or mudroom. Having things out of place in the rest of the house and the resulting inconvenience that it causes may be a good incentive for moving quickly to complete your garage makeover.

These folks had this storage unit delivered to them.

Photo by Theresa Russell

$ Loose Change

When we worked on our garage project, we put our stuff in the yard and covered it with a big plastic tarp. It cost us just the price of the tarp. The tarp protected the things from the weather. If you live in a neighborhood with zoning restrictions, be sure this is permitted.

Get Rid of It

Hanging on forever to everything in the garage is counterproductive to your project. Be sure to ask yourself if you really need a particular item. Is it easily replaceable? Will you ever use it? Could someone else benefit from it? Disposing of your things will likely take a lot more energy than acquiring them took. There are several ways to rid yourself of these no longer needed or wanted items.

Return It

Some of the things you find in your garage probably belong to someone else. Perhaps you borrowed something from the neighbor. Maybe somebody asked you to temporarily store their things in your garage, and "temporarily" has

turned into "permanently." Now is the time to return those borrowed items. Get in touch with those people who have put their things in your garage and ask them to come and get them out. Tell them what your plans are. Maybe they will help you with your project. Maybe you can give them some other things to take with them.

Sell It

Selling your possessions can bring in some extra cash, particularly if your things are desirable. Maybe Grandma's antique bedroom set will never fit your décor, but for somebody else it would be perfectly suitable. Have your kids outgrown their bicycles? Have you switched from mountain biking to road biking? Those spare tires from the car that you traded in years ago could make somebody very happy. What about that old window air conditioner that you used before you installed central air? You can sell things using many different resources—the newspaper classifieds, eBay, craigslist, garage sales, or auctions.

Don't assume that some of the things you find in your garage are worthless. A friend who is a military widow decided to get rid of the boxes of stuff that her husband kept in the garage. She found several boxes of orders that her husband had saved throughout his military career. She was quite familiar with his pack rat ways, but didn't understand why he had to save every single order he or his troop had ever received.

She had put most of these papers out for the garbage, but she found a few interesting things that she took to a local museum for donation. The museum bought everything she brought that day. The museum director told her to hurry back home and get the rest of the papers out of the garbage heap because they were quite valuable.

This is just one side of the coin. It is just as likely that you have some worthless things in your garage that you've been holding on to because of an emotional attachment. Be honest with yourself as you sort through your stuff. Why do you feel the need to keep it?

Each of these possibilities has its own methods for attracting buyers. Call the antique store to get Grandma's dresser appraised. Look in the Wanted to Buy section of the classifieds. Put your antiques on consignment. One man's junk really is another's treasure.

Give It Away

Giving things away often takes less time and energy than organizing a garage sale or listing on eBay. Plenty of organizations are looking for yarn, material, or used tools.

Consider online marketplaces such as Sharing Is Giving (www.sharingisgiving.org) or Freecycle (www.freecycle.org). Participants offer what they have available to give away and other members of the online groups respond privately to the postings.

You absolutely would be surprised at the things people give away and the things that people are looking for. One recent post on our local board was requesting a toilet. Others want things such as old pill bottles or wine bottles for crafty projects. The main mission of the two organizations above is to keep things out of the dump.

Donate your car to charity, and they will tow it away.

Photo by Theresa Russell

Barter

Maybe you can give away something in your garage in exchange for a service or something else that you can use. Maybe a local teenager would be willing to help you clean out your garage in exchange for that nice drum set that has been in the garage for years.

Trash It

Some of the things in your garage are truly junk. If you can't give it away, toss it. There is no reason to keep the outdated computer monitors or hard drives. There are special programs for recycling old computers.

Most things can simply go out in the trash. However, some items, such as *household hazardous waste*, must be disposed of in special ways. You can take that old oil from the last oil change to an oil recycler for disposal. Don't even consider pouring oil or other toxic items down the sink or sewer drain. Call your local facility to learn the proper way to dispose of things.

Following is a list of items that need special consideration for disposal.

Definitions _____

Household hazardous waste (HHW) are products that cannot simply be thrown into the local landfill. Look for the words *caution*, *poison*, or *danger* on the label. The major categories of HHWs are those that are flammable or combustible, explosive or reactive, corrosive and toxic.

Many labels include disposal instructions.

EPA List of Household Hazardous Waste

Cleaning Products
- Oven cleaners
- Drain cleaners
- Wood and metal cleaners and polishes
- Toilet cleaners
- Tub, tile, shower cleaners
- Bleach (laundry)
- Pool chemicals

Indoor Pesticides
- Ant sprays and baits
- Cockroach sprays and baits
- Flea repellents and shampoos
- Bug sprays
- Houseplant insecticides
- Moth repellents
- Mouse and rat poisons and baits

Automotive Products
- Motor oil
- Fuel additives
- Carburetor and fuel injection cleaners
- Air-conditioning refrigerants
- Starter fluids
- Automotive batteries
- Transmission and brake fluid
- Antifreeze

Workshop/Painting Supplies
- Adhesives and glues
- Furniture strippers
- Oil- or enamel-based paint
- Stains and finishes
- Paint thinners and turpentine
- Paint strippers and removers
- Photographic chemicals
- Fixatives and other solvents

Lawn and Garden Products
- Herbicides
- Insecticides
- Fungicides/wood preservatives

Miscellaneous
- Batteries
- Mercury thermostats or thermometers
- Fluorescent light bulbs
- Driveway sealer

Other Flammable Products
- Propane tanks and gas cylinders
- Kerosene
- Home heating oil
- Diesel fuel
- Gas/oil mix
- Lighter fluid

Drive It Home _____

Some local waste and recycling services suggest pouring cat litter into old cans of latex paint. This solidifies the liquid so that the paint can be disposed of as a solid.

If you have construction materials in your garage, you will likely need to dispose of them at a contractors dump or take them to a transfer station.

The Least You Need to Know

- The first step to organization is to get rid of things.
- Use a system to decide what to keep or pitch.
- Hazardous waste requires special disposal.
- One man's junk is another's treasure.

In This Chapter

- ◆ Methods for cleaning your garage
- ◆ Making it sparkle
- ◆ Recommended techniques
- ◆ Safety precautions

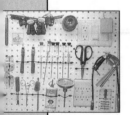

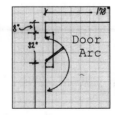

Chapter 7

Down and Dirty

Now that you have everything out of your garage, you may see dirt you never realized was there. Because the garage is all cleared out, the big oil stains on the floor are obvious. The walls look filthy, and the trim around the door seems dirtier than ever.

From the ceiling to the floor, you want to make your garage shine. It is amazing what a little bit of elbow grease does to improve the overall look of your garage.

Get those rubber gloves on and start cleaning.

Clean Top to Bottom

This old adage just makes lots of sense. You want to start at the top because all of that dust and grime you move around has to go somewhere. The law of gravity says that it will go down to the floor or to anything on a lower level.

Walls and Ceilings

Your strategy will differ depending on whether your garage is finished or unfinished. If the ceiling is finished, take a dust mop to remove the surface dirt. If the ceiling still looks dirty, you may want to get up there and wash it down. If you are planning on painting, you need to wash it down anyway in preparation for painting.

Drive It Home

Wash walls and ceiling with *TSP* to prep for painting. Read and follow directions carefully.

If you are cleaning the ceiling or anything else that is high up in the garage, such as the electric door opener, you need a ladder. The following list comes from the Consumer Product Safety Commission. Because many injuries result from unsafe use of ladders, follow their advice:

◆ Make sure the weight your ladder is supporting does not exceed its maximum load rating (user plus materials). There should only be one person on the ladder at one time.

◆ Use a ladder that is the proper length for the job. Proper length is a minimum of 3 feet extending over the roofline or working surface. The three top rungs of a straight, single, or extension ladder should not be stood on.

Definitions

TSP or trisodium phosphate is the cleaner of choice for prepping walls for painting. Mixed with a bit of bleach, it also removes mildew from walls. Wear eye protection and gloves when using it. Don't get it on metal or wood surfaces; it can damage them. Follow the manufacturer's instructions when using this potent cleaner.

◆ Straight, single, or extension ladders should be set up at about a 75-degree angle.

◆ All metal ladders should have slip-resistant feet.

◆ Metal ladders conduct electricity. Use a wooden or fiberglass ladder in the vicinity of power lines or electrical equipment. Do not let a ladder made from any material contact live electric wires.

◆ Be sure all locks on extension ladders are properly engaged.

◆ The ground under the ladder should be level and firm. Large, flat wooden boards braced under the ladder can level a ladder on uneven or soft ground. A good practice is to have a helper hold the bottom of the ladder.

◆ Do not place a ladder in front of a door that is not locked, blocked, or guarded.

◆ Keep your body centered between the rails of the ladder at all times. Do not lean too far to the side while working.

◆ Do not use a ladder for any purpose other than that for which it was intended.

◆ Do not step on the top step, bucket shelf or attempt to climb or stand on the rear section of a stepladder.

◆ Never leave a raised ladder unattended.

◆ Follow use instruction labels on ladders.

The other things to clean at the upper levels of the garage are fans, light fixtures, the garage door opener, and any type of storage units that may be up there.

If you have an unfinished garage, your job is to get the dust and cobwebs off the rafters. If you have a floored or partially floored space above the rafters, you want to work on cleaning that up, too. Don't forget, you already should have emptied it at this point in time.

This is the proper way to use a ladder.

Photo by Theresa Russell

When you finish cleaning the ceiling, you can move to the walls. You do pretty much the same things here. Remove the dust and cobwebs, clean the windows if there are any, and clean any other surfaces. Again, there should be nothing on any surface, because you already cleared all that stuff out (so that you could give the garage a thorough cleaning). If your walls are simply studs or concrete, you may just want to remove the surface dirt. For a finished wall, you may want to wash it down to prep it for painting, or just dust it off and spot clean dirty areas.

Floor

The floor is probably the dirtiest place in your garage, if not the whole house. Just think of all the dirt that gets tracked in there. Not only does dirt from your shoes get in there, but so does dirt from your car. If the car has been driven in the rain, mud, or snow, it will drop its residual filth onto the floor. If the car is leaking any fluids, they will go to the floor.

Your floor is likely concrete, which is a porous material, so all that dirt just seeps into its pores. One way to prevent this problem in the future is to paint or seal the floor. But for now we are concentrating on simply cleaning it.

Use a strong cleaner and get as much dirt off the floor as possible. Start in the back of the garage and work toward the door. Use the garden hose to wash the remaining dirt out into the driveway. Cleaning the floor can be a challenge, but some techniques make it easier.

Stain Removal

Oil and other greasy stains can be a real pain to remove.

For a tough oil stain, use dishwasher detergent or cat litter to soak up some of the residue.

Loose Change

A janitor at the school where Robert taught used toilet bowl cleanser to remove oil stains from the parking lot.

You don't need to buy anything special for your garage floor.

Put a bunch directly on the oil stain. Get a dry brush or broom with stiff bristles and scrub the area.

Powerwashing

Powerwashing, also known as pressure washing, can be very dangerous. It can also be an environmental hazard.

Warning Light _____

Be careful with powerwashers. Keep them away from your appendages; they can do major damage. Also don't get too close to your target as you wash the garage; a powerwasher can work away at brick and cement, leaving more of a mess than when you started.

Although it does clean very well, be sure that you follow all instructions if you decide on this cleaning method.

Products and Tools

You can find many products on the market for cleaning. Sometimes finding the product that works best is a matter of trial and error. Check out the products at your local home improvement store to see the selection of cleansers available. Always try to go with the least-toxic cleaner first. Some of the more powerful cleaners contain *volatile organic compounds* (VOCs), which can cause your eyes to burn, your throat to hurt, and the garage to smell.

Definitions _____

VOCs, **volatile organic compounds**, are emitted gases from certain solid and nonsolid compounds. Often they are found in cleaning and other everyday products. Some examples include paint, building materials, pesticides, permanent markers, and correction fluid. They may have both short- and long-term adverse effects on your health. Some VOCs are known or suspected carcinogens.

Cleaners with solvents aren't the smartest products to use, especially if there are appliances with pilot lights in your garage. You are going for something gentler, because you just disposed of all the hazardous chemicals in your garage. Right? No matter what you use, be sure to have plenty of fresh air circulating in the garage while you are cleaning.

Wearing a mask will help you breathe easier.

Photo by Theresa Russell

Another cleaner that doesn't require the use of chemicals is a steam cleaner. Using high-pressure steam, a steam cleaner can help dissolve stubborn stains. Be careful you don't burn yourself while using it, though. It can be extremely hot.

Safety

Even though getting that garage sparkling clean is important, safety should be your first concern. Be sure that all your equipment is in good working order. Wear a mask to keep the dust out of your lungs. Use one with a *HEPA filter* for the best protection, and use HEPA filter bags in your shop vacuum cleaner. Put on eye protection to keep particles of dirt from getting into them and protect them from cleaning solvents. When you clean, put on gloves and leave the doors and windows open to get adequate ventilation. Be careful on that ladder.

Definitions

HEPA filters, or high-efficiency particulate air filters, are considered the ultimate filters. They trap particles as small as .3 microns with an efficiency of 99.97 percent. This is the dust mask to wear when cleaning. These filters also work in vacuum cleaners and furnaces.

You may encounter bees or wasps in your garage. Have a can of hornet spray handy. Read and follow instructions carefully. You may see evidence of mice. After you scream, chase the mouse (or mice) with a broom until it (or they) leaves the garage. This will add an aerobic element to your cleaning day. Look for the access

hole. If one exists, stuff it with a steel wool pad for now. Seal it when you are working on your garage.

You also may find yourself in close company with squirrels, bats, birds, or other creatures. Climbing a ladder and trying to shoo away a flying guest is asking for trouble. Don't do it. If you are frequently shooing pests away, it is time to call a pest control expert.

The Least You Need to Know

- ◆ Clean thoroughly before starting any other project.
- ◆ Use care and common sense when cleaning.
- ◆ Wear proper safety equipment.
- ◆ Read labels and follow the instructions.
- ◆ Do everything with safety in mind so you get to the next chapter.

In This Chapter

- ◆ Taking stock of the inside of your garage
- ◆ Taking stock of the outside of your garage
- ◆ Inspecting the garage for problems
- ◆ Using the checklist

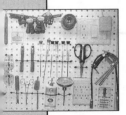

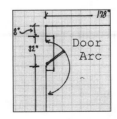

Chapter 8

Assessing the Structure

You have cleared everything out of your garage. You cleaned the garage from top to bottom. Now let's figure out what you have left. You can easily get to any area now to measure, to plan, and to look for problems that need to be addressed before you put your car and stuff back in. In this chapter, you work through a series of questions and use the checklist at the end of the chapter to record answers and measurements. The more you know about your garage, the better off you will be when planning and designing your solution.

You may want to consider hiring a trained and experienced house inspector. The inspector's report should provide the details about the construction of your garage. This information will help make you an informed consumer when you start looking for ways to repair or improve your garage. If you already plan on hiring a contractor to upgrade your garage or install some storage system, that contractor should be able to do an adequate inspection for you.

Inside Your Garage

Before you start hanging shelves or storage units, it is easier to take care of any structural problems with your garage. Be sure that walls will safely support whatever you plan to hang on them. If you plan to use attic space, confirm that the structure can bear the load of a second floor. Let's start by taking a look at the walls.

Drive It Home _____

The American Society of Home Inspectors is the most widely recognized organization of inspectors. ASHI members must meet certain requirements and adhere to the ASHI Code of Ethics and Standards of Practice.

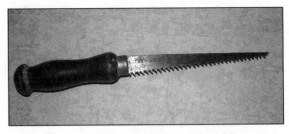

The keyhole saw has a sharp point for jabbing into drywall.

Photo by Theresa Russell

Walls

Walls are made from a variety of materials. Typically, you should find a wooden framework covered on the exterior by *sheathing* and siding or masonry. On the interior, you should find some type of sheathing if the garage is finished. You could have steel studs or concrete block walls rather than a wooden frame.

Definitions _____

Sheathing is any type of wall covering used on the exterior or on the interior of a house. It frequently refers to exterior-grade sheets of plywood.

The size of your wall studs may vary depending on when your garage was built. If your garage is unfinished, they should be easy to measure. Typically, you should find 2"×4" or 2"×6" studs. The 2"×4" studs have actual measurements of 1" on the exposed end and 3" on the side connecting to the outside sheathing. The 2"×6" likewise measure 1" by 5". If your garage is finished, you have a couple of options for obtaining measurements. If you have drywall, you can use a keyhole saw to cut a small observation hole that can be patched later.

You also can measure indirectly by looking at a window or doorframe and subtracting the thickness of the interior and exterior wall coverings and trim from the total thickness.

Drive It Home _____

Why does a 2"×4" measure less than 2"×4"? The rough-sawn lumber starts out approximately 2"×4"; however, after planing and sanding, it measures a standard 1"×3".

Current code requires that studs be a certain distance apart. Older garages, especially, were not always built to code. You need to find out how far apart the studs are. We look at a variety of ways to find out that distance.

If the walls are unfinished, you can simply measure the spacing. The studs should be placed 16" to 24" on center (from the center of one stud to the center of the next one).

If your walls are covered, you may be able to see evidence of the fastening patterns indicating the stud spacing. Look for the fasteners themselves, or, if they have been hidden by joint compound, look for the pattern created by joint compound covering nails. If the walls have been painted, look for the dimples or depressions where the fasteners are hidden.

These wall studs are 2"× 6"s placed 16" on center.

Photo by Mary Mihaly

A crude technique for finding studs behind finished walls is to drill a series of small holes until you find one and then move 16" horizontally and hope to find the next one.

![Warning Light icon] **Warning Light** _____

Before you begin drilling holes in the wall, try to determine whether there are any pipes, electrical wires, or ducts in the wall. If there is evidence that there might be, such as a receptacle or sink nearby, don't risk damaging them with the drill.

A less-destructive technique is to use an electronic or sonic stud finder. When you have located the studs, mark their edges. You need their location for mounting many types of storage devices.

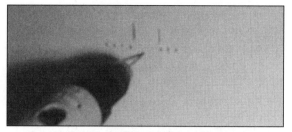

Not the most elegant way to find studs, but it is effective.

Photo by Theresa Russell

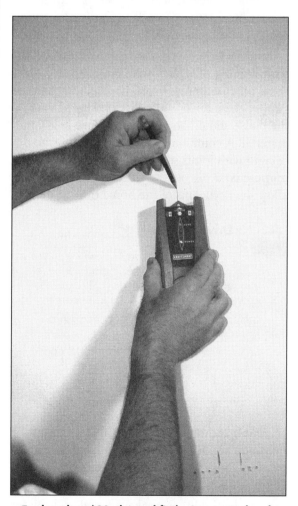

For less than $30, the stud finder is a pretty handy tool. Notice that you can quickly and efficiently mark the edges of the studs.

Photo by Theresa Russell

Now that you know how far apart your studs are, you need to know what is in between the studs. Sometimes walls are insulated and not covered in a garage. That makes it pretty easy to see. If the walls are covered, maybe you can see the insulation or the lack of it in the observation hole you made previously. Otherwise, it may be difficult to determine the existence and condition of any insulation without some detection equipment.

Garages come with all sorts of wall coverings or "self-covered" walls (as is the case with cement block garages).

Interior walls in a garage can be sheathed with drywall, paneling, plywood, pegboard, or some other material. If you have an attached garage, the interior walls that are shared with the house should be covered by a fire-resistant material. A common material is 5/8" type X drywall with joints sealed using fire tape. The purpose is to restrict the spread of fire and allow the occupants of the home time to escape.

Drive It Home

If you find a couple of layers of drywall in your garage, it may not have been from a past remodeling job. Two layers of regular drywall have been used as a fire-resistant barrier. This application does meet building code requirements in some areas. Always check with your local code enforcement agency for updates on the code in your area.

Your measurements and visual inspection may indicate that you have some concerns or problem areas to deal with.

If you can see the studs, look for loose, missing, cracked, split, or weakened studs. Check for water and insect damage, especially along the floor and ceiling. Is there any loose or damaged sheathing?

If you have concrete block walls, look for soft or missing mortar joints. Also look for cracks and missing blocks or missing parts of blocks. Are there cracks, flaking, or *efflorescence?*

Definitions

Efflorescence is a white, powdery substance cause by water leaking through a solid surface such as concrete, brick, or tile. It is caused by the residual salts from the water as it passes through to the surface.

Ceiling

Your ceiling may be open rafters or may be finished with drywall, tiles, or another covering. Your garage ceiling is constructed of a wooden framework of horizontal joists that may be part of a roof truss system. It may be separate or may be the underside of the attic floor joists. If the garage is finished, there should be some type of interior sheathing.

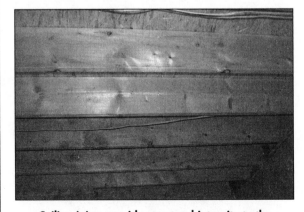

Ceiling joists provide structural integrity to the garage.

Photo by Theresa Russell

Just like the wall studs, ceiling joists have certain standard placement. If your ceiling is not covered, you can easily measure the joists. They should be 2" × something, actually measuring 1" by anywhere from 3" to 11". If the ceiling is covered, you may have access to the joists from an attic space or a bathroom plumbing access panel. Otherwise, you may want to use one of the techniques described previously for measuring wall studs.

The spacing should be 16" to 24" *on center*. This measurement along with the size of the joists is crucial to determining what kind of load the ceiling can support for your storage solution.

Definitions _____

The distance between two structural members, measured from the center of one to the center of the adjacent one, is **on center**.

You may have an uncovered ceiling with insulation. That's easy to assess. Or you may be looking at drywall. Did you see any insulation while measuring the joists? With no access to the space above the drywall, it can be difficult to assess the existence or condition without making a hole in the ceiling.

This garage is finished with drywall.

Photo by Schulte

Drywall is typically the most common sheathing used in finished garages. If the garage is attached, the ceiling should be covered completely with a fire-resistant material, as discussed earlier. You may have a garage that has some other covering, such as plywood, fiberboard, paneling, or ceiling tile.

Look for the same things that you did when inspecting the wall. If you can see the joists, are there any that are loose, missing, cracked, split, or weakened? Is there evidence of water or insect damage? Is there loose or damaged sheathing? Does the ceiling sag appreciably anywhere?

If there is an overhead garage door and opener, are the supports in good shape? You may want to have a professional garage door service evaluate the entire system.

Floor

Garage floors are most often concrete, but some older garages have dirt floors. We have even seen tiled and carpeted floors. If you have a concrete floor, what is its condition? Are there cracks, flaking, or efflorescence? Is there separation from the foundation? Is the floor drain clogged? You may want to test it by pouring a bucket of water into it.

Windows and Doors

Is the entry door into the house from an attached garage a fire-rated door? If it is not, you should strongly consider replacing it. Check to see that all doors and windows are weather tight, leak resistant, and secure.

If your garage is not getting enough natural light, think about adding a window or putting in doors with windows.

A separate outside entrance in addition to the large garage door makes access to the exterior simpler and quicker than opening the big door.

Definitions _____

Glazing is the glass in the window. Double-glazed windows have two layers of glass.

Warning Light _____

Some building codes require the entry door to be solid wood or steel with a certain fire rating. The fire rating is usually measured in minutes, determined by how long it would take a fire to burn through the door. There may be additional requirements for the door to be self-closing and self-latching.

Check to see whether the doors and windows open and close properly. They should lock and seal adequately without force.

Outside Your Garage

Take a walk around the outside perimeter of the garage and evaluate the condition from top to bottom. Not only will you notice any problems from this vantage point, but you also can see the effects of structural problems by examining the outside components.

Roof

The lines of the roof should look straight and level. A roof can sag as the result of different issues. Some may require attention, and others may be from settling that stabilized long ago. A structural engineer may need to be called for serious problems, such as serious roof sags, significant separation of structural members, major rot, and deterioration.

How are the shingles? When a garage is attached, the garage roof is almost always reroofed with the rest of the house. If the garage is detached, the roof might have been neglected. Shingles vary in quality and in their length of useful service. They can last from 15 to 40 years. Look for signs of deterioration, such as curling, warping, or rounded corners. Slate roofs can last 75 years or much longer.

Tile and metal roofs also can last a long time depending on quality and maintenance.

Take a good look at the outside of your garage.
Photo by John Rider

Look for any conditions that might lead to leaks. Pay particular attention to broken or missing shingles and loose or missing *flashing*.

Look for loose or missing sections and visible rot on the *soffit* and *fascia*. We once had a loose soffit section that a raccoon discovered while climbing on the roof. He promptly made himself a home in the attic insulation. He was an unwelcome tenant and not easy to evict.

Definitions _____

Sheet metal used to reinforce and weatherproof the joints and angles of a roof is called **flashing**.

The **soffit** is the horizontal covering of the rafter extensions that form the eave.

Fascia is the vertical trim that covers the ends of the rafters.

Make sure that the gutters and downspouts are clean and have the proper slope. Look for loose or missing sections. Make sure the downspouts are not clogged and extend away from the foundation. I once worked on a house where the downspout extension had come loose. The rainwater collecting along the foundation caused uneven settling, and the attached garage started to pull away from the house, leaving a 1-inch gap in the ceiling above the garage.

Foundation

Take note of anything unusual or bad around the foundation.

Check for cracks, shifting, or settling. Look for soft or missing mortar. Check for bulging or other irregularities. Look for insect tubes or other animal activity.

Siding

The exterior of your garage is likely finished with some sort of siding or is brick or masonry. Check around for loose or missing pieces of siding. Look and see if the mortar between the bricks or blocks is soft or missing. Note the condition of the walls. Bowing, bulging, and leaning are conditions that might warrant a call to a structural engineer. Check for rot, mildew, and discoloration.

Garage Door

If you regularly park your car in the garage, the garage door sees lots of wear and tear. Does the garage door appear level and properly spaced in its opening?

Does the door sag?

Can you open and close the garage door easily without having it drag or need to be lifted or tilted into its closed position?

Is the hardware in good condition?

Check the hinges, tracks, rollers, and opener hardware if applicable.

Warning Light

Garage door maintenance and safety testing is one of the most commonly neglected tasks of homeowners. Photoelectric eyes have been required since 1993, reversing mechanisms have been required since 1991, and emergency disconnects became standard in 1982. Is your opener up-to-date? The Consumer Product Safety Commission recommends a monthly testing of the safety systems.

Are all safety features installed and functioning properly?

A garage door is probably the largest and heaviest moving part of your home. Three safety features should be tested regularly. The safety reverse beam should be installed 4 to 6 inches off the floor. When the beam is broken, the direction of the door should reverse. The auto-reverse sensor should reverse the direction of the door either when an object is encountered in the path of the door or when the door encounters moderate resistance in either direction. The last safety feature is the safety counter balance spring. With the door in the closed position, disconnect the opener by tripping the release mechanism. You should be able to open the door with little effort and it should remain balanced at the half-open position.

Problems with the first two tests may be corrected by adjustments detailed in the owner's manual or by the replacement of an older unit. If your door fails the third test, the balance tension should be adjusted only by a qualified service professional. The balance springs are under significant tension and can cause serious injury during adjustment.

Garage doors come in many styles.

Photo by Clopay

The Inspection Checklist

Use this checklist to keep track of your findings. Hold on to it for future reference.

Interior

Walls

Frame

Stud Dimensions ___×___

Stud Spacing ____ o.c.

Insulation

Type _____

Thickness _____

Sheathing

Type _____

Thickness _____

Problems or Concerns

_____

_____

Ceiling

Frame

Joist Dimensions ___×___

Joist Spacing ____ o.c.

Insulation

Type _____

Thickness _____

Problems or Concerns

_____

_____

Floor

Condition _____

Drain _____

Windows and Entry or Interior Doors

Window

Open-Close _____

Seal _____

Lock _____

Door

Open-Close _____

Seal _____

Lock _____

Exterior

Roof

Shingles

Age _____

Signs of Deterioration

_____

Evidence of Leaks

_____

Gutters and Downspouts

_____

Overhangs

_____

Potential Problems

_____

_____

Foundation

Problems or Concerns

_____

_____

Siding

Problems or Concerns

_____

_____

Garage Door

Condition _____

Hardware _____

Operation _____

Safety

Safety Reverse Beam _____

Auto-Reverse Sensor _____

Safety Counter Balance Spring _____

The Least You Need to Know

- Know where the garage studs and rafters are.
- Fix problems before beginning your new project.
- Check the garage door safety features monthly.
- Make sure the safety features of the garage door all function properly.

In This Chapter

- ◆ Reevaluating your new space
- ◆ Taking stock of your needs
- ◆ Inspecting the garage for problems
- ◆ Using all available space

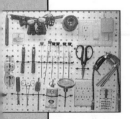

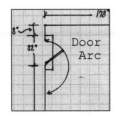

Design Your Space

Now that you have your garage cleaned out and everything updated and repaired, step back and see what you have to work with. Keep in mind that making a few simple changes can go a long way in making your garage work for you. When you think about what to put in your garage, you have to allow space for doors opening, walking around the car and other items, and getting in and out of the car.

There may be a few things you could change that would help your garage function better. Maybe the outside door is in a poor location. If your garage needs a bit of light on it, you can do a few things to improve it. You can either add more natural light or install electrical lighting. Let's start designing your space.

Step Back and Reevaluate

Your garage is empty. Do you recognize it? Do you have some ideas for it? Are they simple or complicated? Maybe you imagined that you had much more space than you really do, or did the garage seem smaller with all the stuff jammed into it? It is easy to misjudge distances from doors to windows and along walls. Once again, think about the main purpose of your garage.

Look at all this empty space.

Photo by Gladiator

Drive It Home

An uncluttered room lets energy flow. When you are thinking about what to do with your space, you don't need to fill every single bit of emptiness. Too much clutter is an obstacle to fresh energy—and an obstacle to prosperity, new possibilities, and new beginnings that want to "enter" the space.

—Mary Mihaly, Feng Shui consultant

Now that you see it in its clean splendor, maybe you want to keep it this way and store only the car in there. On the other hand, maybe it looks perfect for a home office. By now, you have probably looked at some websites, books, or magazines to see what is out there. You will start with the simple solutions. If you have plans for bigger projects, you can read about them in Chapters 13 and 14.

Plan a Place for Everything

You've planned all the other things involved with this garage up to this point. Don't stop planning. Planning is critical for finding a place for everything. Sit down and think about what you have left in that "keep" box or pile.

Do you see a pattern? Do you have mostly garden tools or handyman tools to store? Is more of your stuff seasonal? Do you have bunches of tiny things that can be stored

together? Or do you have a bit of everything? Is anything temperature sensitive?

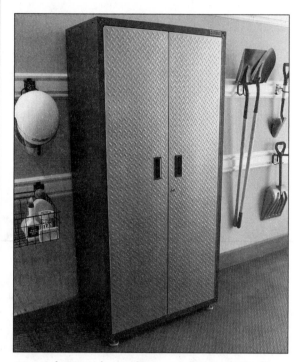

Bigger things such as cabinets need to be on the floor.

Photo by Gladiator

Look between your studs and on the wall for space.

Photo by Hyloft

Up, up, and away.

Photo by Hyloft

Another way to get things off the floor.

Photo by Hyloft

You've heard it before. You have three places for storage: floor, wall, and ceiling. Garage organizers suggest that you keep everything off the floor, but you may want to keep some things there.

> **Warning Light** _____
>
> Be sure your garage can handle extra weight. Sagging joists indicate a problem. Don't add to it by hanging things from them. This is a disaster in the making.

Just be sure that your newfound storage doesn't get in the way of the car. The wall has lots of space, and many of the things you put there might encroach into the main area of the garage. Think about how department stores display their wares. The ceiling also keeps things out of the way, and is a good place if your garage is small. Keep your height and physical limitations in mind when thinking of a place for your things.

Go through the things you are keeping again. Sort your things so that similar things are together (such as kids' toys, seasonal decorations, workbench tools, and so on). A generic sorting technique involves using three groups. After you have grouped your similar objects, divide them into those you use frequently, those you use occasionally, and those seldom used. Objects that are in frequent demand need to be easily accessible, and those that are rarely used can be tucked out of the way. This way, you can get an idea of what you have to store. Make a list of everything so that you also figure out how and where you are going to store everything.

As you are planning your space, you can use graphing paper to lay out your ideas or use a software program to lay them out.

Software

If you are just a bit tech savvy, consider using some software rather than graphing paper to lay out your new plan. You can also consult with some of the experts who have software at their fingertips to illustrate a variety of design layouts that might appeal to you. You don't have to buy their products. You may want to buy just one and substitute different products or your own to complete the look. An example of a site where you can design your space using a specific line of products is www.gladiatorgw.com/BluePrint.

> **$ Loose Change** _____
>
> If you are thinking of installing cabinets in your garage and want to see how they look, go to some free kitchen design software sites online. Just be sure to choose the right-size cabinets for your area. You don't need to fill in the entire room. Of course, your cabinets will look different, but this gives a good idea of how your arrangement will look.

When choosing software, look for something with a short learning curve unless you are considering doing this for a living. Spending big bucks for software that you will use one time is a waste of money.

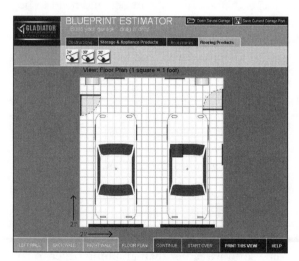

This layout was made using Gladiator's program.

Photo by Gladiator

There are programs for doing layouts, but also for selecting paint colors. This is a perfect way to decide how your garage will look in

a particular color. Most garages seem to be painted white. That and lighter colors are currently in favor, but use whatever color pleases you. It is your garage.

Hooks

Hooks are a quick and cheap way to organize many things. They range from the basic nail in the wall to more fancy coated models. If you are on a budget, consider the good old 10d nail discussed in Chapter 2.

A simple hook makes a difference.

Photo by Coleman

Remember that you can't just pound nails anywhere you want to in the wall. You need to put the hooks in a stud. If you have an unfinished garage with no wall covering, you are in luck. You can see where every single stud is. If your garage has a wall covering, you must go back and review how to find the studs. If you have concrete block walls, your options differ entirely (as addressed in Chapter 10).

Drive It Home

Don't just start installing hooks anywhere. Anchor them on a stud. Toggle bolts don't require a stud and are only good for hanging very lightweight objects. We don't really recommend them. When placing your hooks, consider their height. If you put a hook too high or low for your reach, it doesn't really serve a purpose.

Look between the studs in an unfinished garage. Hooks on the wider inside part of the stud keep things from protruding too far into the garage. If the item you want to hang doesn't have a predrilled hole, you have two options. If it is practical, drill a hole into your item for easier storage.

Loose Change

Lots of items (sheets, for example) come packaged in plastic bags that make excellent places to store odds and ends. They usually have draw strings or are in a zipped bag. Use these in your garage.

If drilling a hole would weaken or damage the product, just attach it with a bungee cord or rope to the nail. Extension cords, hoses, and pool equipment work well with this system.

Reusing packaging is an economical and practical storage solution.

Photo by Bunjipeg

Warning Light

If the hook sticks out so that it is a constant obstacle or source of injury, it isn't a practical place.

Look up to the ceiling for hooking spots. Hooks come in a variety of styles and sizes.

You can find hooks to grab the frame or wheels of a bicycle or to stack lumber.

Two hooks placed at the correct distance apart can make a spot for storing a ladder, surfboard, *PVC* or other pipes, and other long objects. Pole vault, anyone?

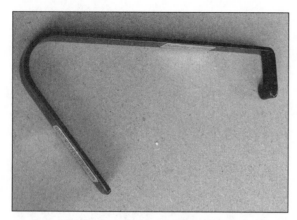

These hooks are made specifically for the garage rail.

Photo by Addahook

 Definitions _____

> **PVC,** polyvinyl chloride, is a plastic used in a variety of building products, such as plumbing pipe, windows, and siding.

Top Shelf

Shelves can hold a larger number of objects in a given space than a set of hooks. Objects can also be more quickly and easily rearranged on shelves. Boxes, containers, and odd-shaped objects are more easily stored on shelves.

Shelves require some of the same installation techniques as hooks do. Most important, you need to locate the studs or joists in your garage. Once again, the owner of the unfinished garage has it easy and has more options than the person with the finished garage. The area between the studs is a perfect place to install a shelf.

If it is narrow enough, the shelf won't extend into the garage itself. If it is wider than the studs, it still takes up less open space than a shelf hung on a finished wall. Shelves are definitely the way to go for getting larger, flat-bottomed containers off the floor. They can be installed in a variety of ways.

Take advantage of space between the studs.

Photo by T. Russell

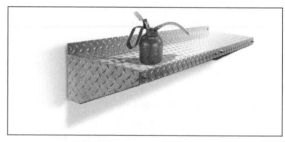

Simple shelves make a big difference.

Photo by Diamondlife

Your simplest option is to buy a free-standing shelf. They come in a variety of materials from industrial metal shelves to plastic shelves. Some models are adjustable in that you can add on layers or take them away as you need them. Others have hardware built in so that you can move the shelves around to your liking.

The freestanding shelf comes in a variety of sizes, so you just need to measure your space and find something with the correct dimensions. These might take a minimal amount of assembly, but you don't have to fool with screwing anything into the walls.

The next type of shelf is a wall-mounted shelf. This works by attaching the shelves to the wall, usually with brackets supporting them. You just buy a rail that screws into the wall and then buy as many shelves as you need. You can place your shelves at appropriate distances depending on the size of the items that you want to store. Again, if you have concrete walls, your options differ. You will find the details in Chapter 10.

This style of shelf attaches to a rail.

Photo by Hyloft

Freestanding shelves are doing the job.

Photo by Diamondlife

Open shelving isn't your only option. Did you just remodel your kitchen and replace the old cabinets? You could easily move them to the garage if you have the space. Paint them to fit the new style of your garage or leave them as they are. They will fit onto either a finished or unfinished wall.

> **$ Loose Change** _____
>
> Don't throw away that old dresser or those old kitchen cabinets yet. Check that they are in good shape and use them in the garage. Paint or stain them to give them a new life in your garage.

Shelves on the ceiling? You can use that dead space between the ceiling joists as a place to put a shelf. There are predesigned models that simply require placement and screwing in the unit. You can also make a shelf just like you did for the space between the wall studs. Remember how you could put two hooks a certain distance apart and put a ladder up there? You can do the same thing. However, put down a board over the hooks and store those things that need a solid surface to sit on. Maybe this is where you put the skis, the camping equipment, or the weed whacker when the weeds quit growing.

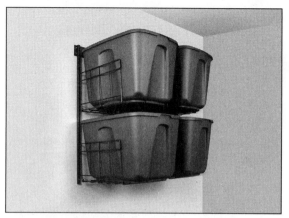

This gets more things off the floor.

Photo by Hyloft

When thinking about shelves or hooks or any system, keep in mind the load limits of whatever you are using. Read and follow the guidelines recommended in the instructions. Don't expect to put a ton of junk on a plastic shelf. You are setting yourself up for disaster and a possible trip to the emergency room.

Short Stack

Next in the progression of storage options is stacking things. Of course, you can stack things on a shelf and that is an excellent idea. You can also stack a group of similar boxes on top of each other. Think of all of those colorful storage bins that you see in the store. You could get some in a variety of colors to help you distinguish their contents. Small toolboxes with recessed handles stack easily, as do those little sets of plastic drawers. These are perfect for smaller items that can be grouped together but are so small that they don't demand a storage container of their own.

Drive It Home

When stacking containers, label the outsides to speed up your search for items.

You can stack things on a workbench, on the floor, on a shelf, or even in the joists or attic. Measure the space that you have. Don't expect to shove everything into one big container. Unless all the items are related, it is better to have a separate container for each category of stuff that you have. Storing the sleeping bags in the same big container as the holiday decorations doesn't make a whole lot of sense. Get two smaller containers.

Remember to stack the heaviest things at the bottom of the pile. Don't put so much into a container that lifting it or moving it around causes physical issues. Keep the most frequently used items in the most accessible spot on the pile or shelf.

Nooks and Crannies

If you are short on extra space in your garage, consider some of the nooks and crannies that you can use. Have you looked at the space above the garage door? Be sure that there is enough space there to keep the garage door functioning properly. There is always space on the back of entry doors. Think about putting some sort of over-the-door storage there. A hook or a shoe bag, which can be used for more than just shoes, will work well there.

If your windows have a deep enough sill, you might be able to put shelves in front of the window. If your car almost touches the end wall of your garage, don't despair. Put a shelf on the back wall, but put it higher than the hood of the car. The return of the garage is also an often overlooked place for storing items.

Maybe there is a place on the outside of your garage for storage. Can you hang a rack on the exterior wall for the garden hose? Look at all the spaces you have that at first don't seem obvious. You surely will find a place that you had overlooked.

Warning Light _____

If you hang anything on the outside of the garage, be sure that the way in which it is attached doesn't ruin the integrity of the exterior sheathing. Putting holes into siding might not be a good idea.

A corner shelf takes up little space.

Photo by Hyloft

Storage Solutions

With the increase in the number of people organizing their garages, new products and innovative storage solutions are coming onto the market regularly. There are complete storage solutions with mix-and-match items for completing your project. Many of the manufacturers or retailers of these solutions have representatives or independent contractors who will

gladly sit down with you and help you come up with a design. Other manufacturers have their own proprietary system. Those include slatted wall systems such as those offered by Gladiator and GarageTek. See Appendix D for contact information.

The slats are the base for hanging different objects.

Photo by Gladiator

The first complete systems would be analogous to kitchen cabinets. All the different styles and models are there. You just need to know what you want for your garage. Some of the makers of these products, such as Closet Maid, do custom solutions for you. Don't think, though, that all these products are high-end, custom-ordered deals.

Loose Change _____

When retail stores go out of business, they often sell their fixtures. This is an ideal place to find a slat wall system or other types of items to attractively organize your garage. Be sure to bring your measurements and take a measuring tape along with you to the sale.

You can go into your friendly discount store and find a wide variety of storage systems. Usually the manufacturers have online examples of how to use their systems. Check out the layout examples online, in the store, and in the manufacturers' brochures to get ideas for designs.

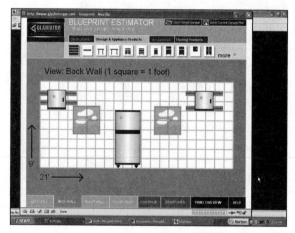

This planner is helpful for getting an idea about how your garage will look with different items.

Photo by Gladiator

The slat wall system is one that basically consists of slats installed horizontally along your garage wall. You buy different accessories to hang from the slats. You can buy as many or as few slats or accessories as you want. You can easily rearrange and change your design as your needs change. When the system is installed, you have a variety of options.

Another system is the rail system. In this system, you get rails to which you attach your storage accessories. You then just attach the types of accessories you want to the rails.

These work for any kind of garage, but concrete garage owners need to take some extra steps to get this system working. See Chapter 10 for instructions.

You don't need to do an entire wall with this system.

Photo by Schulte

On Clearance

Clearance is the buzzword for designing your system. If you can't park the car in the garage because a cabinet is in the way, your system won't work. Find your drawing of the car and the car with the doors opened. Look at the arc of any other interior or exterior doors. Check out the furnace or other utilities. They must be accessible. Be sure to leave enough space around anything that has a pilot light. If it turns out that something will bump into something else, rethink your plans. Don't get discouraged yet. Be glad that you have addressed this problem before you have spent any money.

There are parking guides that help you park your car in a regular space. This product can make it easy for you to know where to park your car so that your storage systems are accessible and have enough clearance for their parts to work.

You'll park in the same spot every time with this helper.

Photo by Diamondlife

If you have little space, you might want to install some type of system knowing full well that you will have to park the car outside the garage to fully take advantage of the system. This might be fine for certain storage solutions. However, if this is what you need to do to access whatever is stored, be sure that you realize how much extra effort it will take. If this isn't a problem or concern to you, go for it. It is your system and you need to do what works for you. On the other hand, if you don't want to bother moving the car just to get to the snow shovel, think of a different layout.

In Appendix E, we have provided some generic garage floor plan sketches with which you can do some planning. Find the one that most closely matches your garage. Modify it as necessary to place doors, windows, and other features on the sketch. We have also provided some graph paper with which you can sketch your garage if the ones we provided simply didn't come close. Also, you can use the graph paper to represent large items such as lawn tractors, storage cabinets, and sports equipment. Sketch a footprint on the graph paper for each of these, cut them out with scissors, and shuffle them around on your garage floor plan sketch to find the most efficient location for each.

When you think you have your layout, go into the garage and put masking tape around the outline of everything you plan to keep in the garage. See how much space you have for clearance.

Beautify Your Space

You have just a few things to store or a ton to store, but you think your garage is just too plain and ugly. You already have improved its appearance by clearing it out and scrubbing it down. However, you have several options for making it more aesthetically pleasing.

First, a fresh coat of paint can do wonders for giving the garage a new, clean look. This works on both finished and cement block garages. Just be sure that you get the right type of paint for your surface.

Here are some examples of paint terms you may encounter:

- **Latex.** Uses a water-based vehicle to carry the pigment and solids that produce the skin or coating
- **Gloss.** The amount of sheen the final finish will have
- **Oil.** Uses a solvent or oil-based vehicle to carry the pigment and solids that produce the skin or coating
- **Enamel.** A type of paint that dries having a durable, hard, glossy finish

Because the garage walls and doors take a beating, consider using something other than flat paint, which is more difficult to clean.

You've chosen your color and purchased your paint. Your next task is to prepare the walls, ceiling, and floor. Wall paint, ceiling paint, and floor paint are each at least a little different from one another in terms of coverage and may be very different in terms of durability. Read each paint can label carefully and follow the instructions. Basically, you need to clean, prepare, and prime the surface before applying the paint. Cleaning the surface usually involves TSP (trisodium phosphate) or a similar cleaner recommended by the manufacturer. Prepping the surface means repairing any cracks or holes. Stain-covering products hide marks on the walls. Most manufacturers recommend a prime coat before painting to promote good adhesion of the paint coat.

Another way to improve the appearance of your garage is to paint the floor. Again, be sure that you use the more durable floor paint specifically made for floors. Or put down a new surface. These solutions are addressed in a later chapter. Painting the floor is quick and easy as long as you have properly prepped the floor. Resurfacing it will take a bit longer, but the results will be long-lasting.

The entrance to your house from your garage is likely the one you use the most often, especially if your garage is attached and you have an automatic garage door opener. Check to see whether there are things to do that can improve the appearance. A fresh coat of paint on the door and the trim around it will brighten up the place in no time. A welcoming doormat or umbrella holder next to the door will add a homey touch.

Structural Modifications

A few structural changes can make your garage a more efficient and pleasant space for you. These include improving the lighting situation, either with additional electrical lights or by adding windows. Moving and replacing doors can make your garage more usable, as can eliminating a door. Some other additions, such as adding running water, can make your garage function more smoothly.

Adding Light Naturally or Electrically

A well-lit garage is a safe garage. Is your garage safe?

Adding light can be as easy as adding more light fixtures or adding fixtures that take higher-wattage bulbs. This is an easy matter if you have plenty of outlets and adequate electric service. Don't even think of getting a giant extension cord to run every single light in the garage from. Adding more outlets or upgrading service is covered in Chapter 16.

Natural light is always nice and can be done in a few ways. You could either add new windows to the walls or put in skylights on the roof.

Replacing solid doors with doors containing windows is a simple job that can also add some architectural detail to your garage.

Doors with windows add natural light.

Photo by Overhead

Both will take some structural modifications if they aren't already there. If you already have a spot for a window or just need to replace glass, that is a much easier project.

Moving or Replacing Doors

Do you keep trying to plan that new home office for the garage, but keep running into a doorway that will prevent the right-size counter from being added? Does one of the doors just not open in the right place? This can be either a door into the house or an exterior door.

Moving the door that goes into the house needs real consideration because it effects both the garage and the room it goes into. Maybe there is plumbing or other mechanical components in the wall that would be affected.

Notice the change in appearance with this new door.

Photo by Clopay

You must consider many things before making this move. The outside door might be an easier one to move because the walls most likely don't have utilities running through them. That is not always the case. You can get a contractor to tell you. Again, moving and replacing anything in a frame structure is a whole lot easier than with a concrete block structure. You might just need to stick with artificial lighting for the concrete block structure.

Conveniences

Lots of products can add convenience to your lifestyle. A space for a recycling bin in the garage will free up space in the kitchen. Especially if there are stairs from the house to the garage, having the bin in the garage will save you from carrying the full bin up or down stairs. Other conveniences include touchpads for entering the garage. Some newer garage door openers install on the wall of the garage. Installing these frees up some ceiling space and make it possible to add some more storage there.

Other conveniences include sinks, showers, toilets, central temperature control, motion-detector lights, automatic garage door openers, entertainment systems, and ramps. Save a space for these and read the next few chapters to see what they involve. Your solution will become a more involved product when you add any of these features.

Quick temperature control solutions include adding portable baseboard heat or radiators. This is a matter of simply plugging in the appliance to an outlet. It isn't so simple if you don't have electricity in your garage or don't have adequate electrical service in your garage.

Window air conditioners, fans, and swamp coolers are easy to install. In some neighborhoods where a window air conditioner is not permitted, fans and swamp coolers will have to do. Adding central air is covered in Chapter 16.

The Least You Need to Know

- Use wall and ceiling space effectively.
- Use graph paper or software to lay out your design.
- Software makes it easy to change designs without having to redraw an entire layout as with graph paper.

In This Part

Part 3

The Basic Plan

You've sorted all that excess stuff in your garage. Now you need a place to put it. You know that you need shelves and cabinets. Maybe you're even leaning toward a particular brand or style. We take you on a tour to show you all your options in detail. We look at conventional systems that have worked well over the years. We introduce you to some of the new and exciting products, too.

We tell you how to install it and whether you should do it yourself or have somebody do it for you. You are also going to see very specific solutions for specific purposes such as car care, lawn and garden, toys and sports. You will also learn to safely store hazardous materials in your garage. This section ends with suggestions for a home maintenance center stocked with everything to keep your garage and the rest of your home in top working order.

In This Chapter

- ◆ Options for your walls
- ◆ Keeping everything off the floor
- ◆ Simple storage solutions
- ◆ Newfangled options
- ◆ Put down a floor above the joists

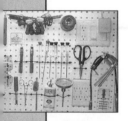

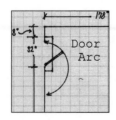

Chapter 10

Beyond the Car

You have your space ready to go. You know exactly where you will park your car. If you park it in the garage, at least it will take up some space, which will prevent you trying to store something in the middle of the floor. Remember that it is never too late to start new habits. Think twice before putting stuff on the garage floor, even if just temporarily. Look how often temporarily turns into a permanent situation.

In this chapter, you learn how to spiff up your garage with simple solutions. You also learn how to install your simple systems that don't require any major structural changes.

Good Old-Fashioned Wall Space

The wall is just waiting for you to put something on it. A fresh coat of paint is an inexpensive way to add new life to your garage.

This section shows you some quick and easy ways to install shelves, pegboard, and cabinets.

Let's take advantage of this wall space.

Photo by Erik Russell

Shelves

Shelves come in all shapes and sizes. You can use cut pieces of lumber, dedicated shelving that is all ready to go, or precut lumber, a good bargain if you don't need something with a brand name on it. If you are using lumber scraps, cut the board to fit the space you have. In addition to the board, you will need some brackets to support it.

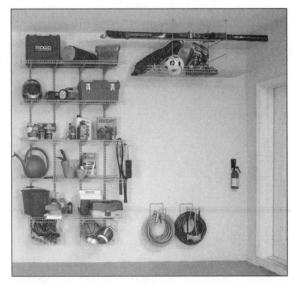

Shelves take up little space but can hold a lot of items.

Photo by ClosetMaid

On a standard wall, the studs are either 16 or 24 inches apart, so you need to install the brackets on the studs. Cut your board a few inches longer than the distance between the studs. Don't allow too much overhang; otherwise, the shelves will dip at the end. Use a level to place your brackets. Draw a line so that you know where to position them.

Drill a pilot hole into the stud. Drive a screw into the studs. This type of system allows you to simply set your piece of wood across the brackets and you have an instant shelf.

Here are the simple instructions for hanging a bracket.

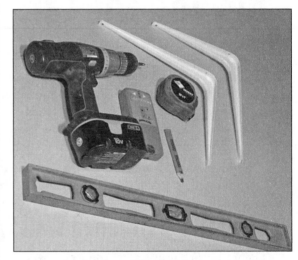

A couple of different brackets and some tools for installing the shelves.

Photo by Schulte

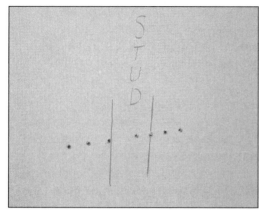

You've located the stud, now place the bracket on the wall and mark where to drill the pilot holes.

Photo by Theresa Russell

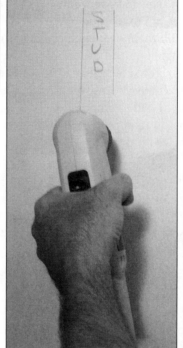

Drill pilot holes using a 1/8" bit, making sure you are penetrating the stud and avoiding any electrical circuits, plumbing pipes, or ductwork.

Photo by Theresa Russell

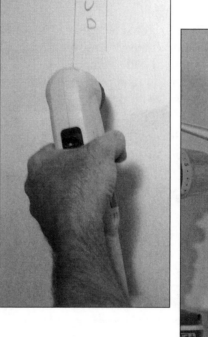

Install the bracket using 2" screws.

Photo by Theresa Russell

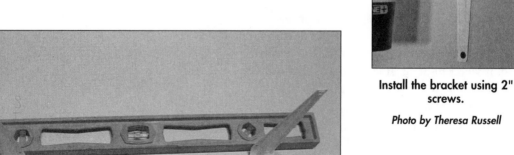

Use a level to locate the position for the next bracket, and repeat the previous steps.

Photo by Theresa Russell

If you have an unfinished garage, you can do the same thing.

Moreover, you also have the option of putting the shelf in between the studs. When we moved into one of our homes, we had an unfinished garage where one wall had these little shelves tucked in between the studs. They went from floor to ceiling, and I didn't think much about them. I proceeded to fill them over time with paint cans, car parts, engine oil and other car fluids, boxes of nails and screws, bicycle parts, and lots of other stuff. It wasn't until we were packing up to move and I had to empty those shelves that I really began to appreciate the volume of storage space on those little shelves.

To take advantage of this space, measure the distance and then cut a piece of wood to fit.

> **$ Loose Change** _____
>
> Remember the adage "Measure twice, cut once." Repeatedly cutting pieces because of inaccurate measuring wastes time and money. Take the extra few seconds to confirm your original measurements.

Slide your piece of wood into the space where you want it. First, be sure that it is the right size. It needs to be a snug fit. If it is too big, it won't fit at all. If it is too small, you won't be able to properly attach it. So slide in your just-right-size board.

Have your level handy. Set it on top of the wood to be sure that it is level. Look at the little bubble in the level to be sure that it is in between the middle lines. When you are sure that your piece of wood is level, make a mark on the top and bottom where it touches the

studs. This will help you drill in the screws in the proper place. With a drill having a $^3/_{16}$" bit, make two clearance holes on each side in between your marks and about $^3/_4$" from the edges.

Change the bit in the drill to a #2 Phillips bit for $2^1/_2$" drywall screws and drive the screw through the back side of the stud. Keep holding your shelf steady and don't let go when you have the first screw in. Drive another screw at the other end. Now repeat the process on the other stud.

Here are some pictures to help you along.

Lots of potential storage space that won't protrude into the room.

Photo by Theresa Russell

A nice snug fit.

Photo by Theresa Russell

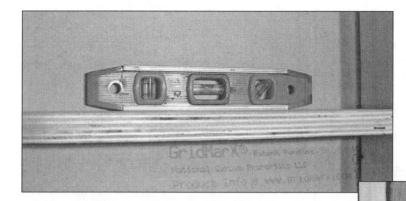

We don't want anything rolling off the shelf.

Photo by Theresa Russell

Draw a line on the studs above and below the board to know where to drill the clearance holes.

Photo by Theresa Russell

Drill two $^3/_{16}$" clearance holes between the lines you just drew about $^3/_4$" from the edge of the stud.

Photo by Theresa Russell

Place the board back in between the marks and secure it with four $2^1/_2$" drywall screws driven through the clearance holes.

Photo by Theresa Russell

Drive It Home

Studs placed 16 inches apart should have a space 14.5 inches between them. Studs placed 24 inches apart should have 22.5 inches between them. (This is assuming that the studs are 2x's.) The depth of a 2×4 is 3.5 inches; the depth of a 2×6 is 5.5 inches. This means that a shelf inserted between 2×6 studs, placed 16 inches on center, would measure 5.5×14.5 inches.

Lumber designated 1×4 and 1×6 for your shelves will have equal corresponding widths to the depths of the 2×4 and 2×6 studs.

If you really, really want to have wall-mounted shelves on your concrete block walls, we consider some ways to do it later in the chapter after we discuss hanging cabinets. Because these are more difficult and time-consuming, we recommend using freestanding shelves instead.

Pegboard

Pegboard is a handy storage solution. You can apply this to both finished and unfinished garages. Once again, it is harder to install on a concrete wall. Find a place on the wall where you want to locate your pegboard. You can buy this in different sizes, including full 4'×8' sheets. If you will be using small pegboards in several spots, consider buying a big sheet and cutting it. It may be more economical. Many lumber suppliers will cut your lumber for you for a minimal cost or no cost at all.

This is an economical way to have many items stored, visible, and easily accessible.

Photo by Alligator Board

If you have an unfinished garage, just install the pegboard. Use a drill with a #2 Phillips bit and $1\frac{1}{2}$" drywall screws. Insert them about 1 foot apart. Drive the screw through the pegboard holes into the studs. Be sure that you buy some hooks and hangers for your pegboard, because this is what will hold up your things.

Drive It Home

Pegboard and hardware come in two grades: normal duty and heavy duty. When you purchase your board and hardware, make sure that they are compatible.

If you have a finished garage, installing a pegboard is a bit more involved. First, you need to install spacers on the walls to allow empty space behind the pegboard where the fasteners will go in. To do this, find the studs and mark them. Use some 1×2 or 1×3 furring strips. Install these right on top of the studs, lining them up parallel to the studs. Use $2\frac{1}{2}$" drywall screws to fasten them down. Next, install the pegboard like we did for the unfinished garage. You also can buy kits that contain mounting screws and spacers that eliminate the need for furring strips.

Hooks, shelves, and containers are just a few ways to utilize your pegboard.

Photo by Alligator Board

Again, buy plenty of pegboard hardware for organizing your stuff. You will be amazed at the variety of options available.

Cabinets

Cabinets come in freestanding and wall-hung models. Freestanding cabinets are the best option for concrete garages. Moreover, they work well for all garages. If you want to hang cabinets, you will go through the same steps you do for hanging shelves. Find the studs, measure for placement, and screw in the cabinets.

One important consideration when installing cabinets is clearance. The doors swing open into space, and if there is something else in that arc, there will be conflict. The hinges may need some clearance, too. Don't put a cabinet so close to a side wall that the door can't swing open the way it should.

Warning Light

If you are reusing your old kitchen cabinets, make sure they are structurally sound. Always drive the mounting screws through the mounting strips on the back of the cabinet. You will find an upper strip and a lower strip. You should use #10 screws of sufficient length to adequately penetrate the studs at least one inch. This means that you will need a $2\frac{1}{2}$- to 3-inch #10 screw to pass through the mounting strip and the drywall and then penetrate the stud. You should use two screws in each stud—one for the upper strip and another for the lower strip.

Be very careful about shoving a cabinet into a tight corner. If you are using old kitchen cabinets, you might consider turning the cabinets into doorless storage if clearance is a problem. Simply remove the doors or remove only the door that doesn't open easily.

You can find lots of cabinet options on the market. They come in plastic, laminate, metal, wood, and composite materials.

Loose Change

Do you know anyone who will be remodeling their kitchen soon? Will they be tossing their old cabinets? Check the want ads for used cabinets. We picked up some cabinets for free on Freecycle. You could find some usable units for little or no cost.

Hung cabinets come in a variety of styles and materials.

Photo by Schulte

More examples of cabinets.

Photo by GarageTek

You could get carried away with installing cabinets.

Photo by Gladiator

Some cabinets have special interiors to organize specific items.

Photo by GarageTek

Installation Challenges

If you happen to have steel studs, engineered joists, concrete block walls, or an unconventional construction in your garage, it is probably best to consider only freestanding storage units. There are many types in a wide price range to choose from.

If have a recently built home with steel stud construction, you can hang shelves, pegboards, slat walls, and cabinets. You need to use fine-thread drywall screws of appropriate length and size to adequately support the brackets, boards, or cabinets. There are also self-drilling screws made especially for fastening to metal. A construction adhesive applied to whatever you are hanging in addition to the screws will help, but it makes the fixture more permanent. Always follow the manufacturer's recommendations, and ask for advice on installation techniques from where you purchase the products.

Another fairly recent construction technique involves *engineered joists*. A garage is a common application for these where long, open expanses are desired while minimizing the need for supporting columns.

![ABC Definitions] **Definitions**

Engineered joists are beams manufactured from wood products using glues and resins to create uniform, stable, and predictable structural components.

Manufacturers of these engineered joists generally state that the structural integrity of their products will be compromised by drilling holes, cutting notches, or installing large screws. If you need to attach a ceiling rack, pulley system, or other storage solution to your ceiling, follow the instructions carefully for attaching to engineered joists. If nothing is mentioned about this type of application, contact the manufacturer or consult your local building department.

Set in Concrete

Concrete block walls confront you with a special challenge for attaching any type of fixture. Your local home improvement center probably has a large section devoted specifically to concrete anchors and fasteners.

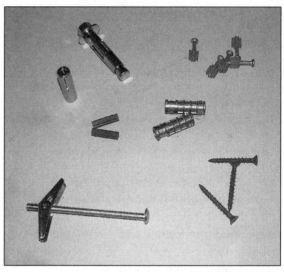

The fasteners are grouped by type. From left to right we have toggle-type, anchors, screws, and nails.

Photo by Theresa Russell

Usually they come in three grades: light, medium, and heavy duty. Carefully read the packages to determine the carrying capacity of each type. Ask the hardware experts for recommendations. They are comparatively much more expensive than the screws used to attach fixtures to studs. There are essentially four different types:

◆ Toggle-type fasteners have spring-loaded arms that expand when they reach an open area behind a hole drilled in the block.

◆ Anchors made of plastic or soft metal are more secure than the wood plugs they evolved from. They are inserted into a hole drilled in the block, and then a screw is driven into them. There are also hammer-set anchors in which a pin is hammered into the anchor rather than a screw.

◆ Concrete screws are driven into a precisely sized hole drilled in the concrete. They are hardened steel and require no anchor.

◆ Hardened nails can be driven into concrete with a power gun that uses gunpowder charges.

Warning Light

A power nail gun for concrete can be a dangerous tool. If you use one, follow all the recommended safety guidelines and observe all the precautions. Some localities regulate their use in construction. Check to see what is available and allowed in your community.

If you choose to use any of the first three, use a hammer drill. If you use a regular drill, you will find drilling concrete block tedious and time-consuming for you and pretty hard on the drill. Don't forget, you must use carbide-tipped bits whenever drilling in concrete.

The only way to drill holes in concrete is with a hammer drill and a carbide-tipped bit.

Photo by Theresa Russell

Here are a few other things to consider. The heavier the load you want to support with the fastener, the larger the diameter and the deeper the penetration into the block. Don't even consider fastening into the mortar joints. You are unlikely to make a secure attachment.

Before you start measuring and marking where to drill the holes, you will need to determine the type of concrete block used in the construction of your garage.

Common types of concrete block.

Photo by Theresa Russell

Typically, hollow blocks with two or three voids were used. You may be able to determine what you have by examining the top of the wall if it isn't sealed or trimmed out. You always can drill a few exploratory holes to determine where the voids are. If 8"×8"×16" or 8"×12"×16" blocks were used, they should be hollow. If smaller blocks were used, they may be solid. You need to use the appropriate fastener for anchoring in the solid part or in the hollow part. I have installed fixtures on concrete block, but I prefer not to because of the extra effort.

A technique that might be a reasonable compromise is to attach a series of wood strips to the concrete block and then attach your shelves, pegboards, and cabinets to those, using the previous techniques. I use 2×4s for heavier loads and 1"×4" furring strips for lighter loads. You can install them vertically or horizontally depending on what will be attached to them. In addition to adequate anchors or fasteners, I use a heavy-duty construction adhesive to ensure they stay put.

You may have a less common type of garage construction such as structural brick walls. It is much more difficult than concrete block to attach to. Or you may have a garage and house built like our daughter's. Her house was built using what is locally known as cottage construction. The walls are built entirely of 1¼"×8" tongue-and-groove boards, no studs, plaster on the inside surface, and batten boards over the outside joints. I was reluctant to attach anything to those walls. Instead, we built new interior walls using a conventional 2×4 framework. This increased the structural integrity of the house and allowed us to insulate and attach cabinets and shelves without concern. This option works almost anywhere. You can build a new wall and design it to match your storage solution.

New and Improved Wall Space

Systems for using your walls for storage space have come a long way. Some of the new systems include specialty pegboards that use bungees, special rail systems, and slat boards. This has made the entire organization process easy. Some of the systems you can install yourself. Others will be professionally installed if you so desire.

Bungees

The bunjipeg system is one that keeps your things stored on a pegboard. The difference between this and a regular pegboard is that you don't need hooks to hold everything. You simply use bungee cords. There's nothing hard about that. The elasticity of the bungee allows the object to easily be removed from the board. The tension in the bungee keeps it right where you want it.

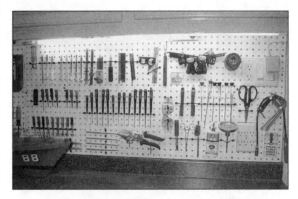

The bunjipeg doesn't require hooks.

Photo by Bunjipeg

You don't need to worry about losing hooks or finding just the right-size hook. Bungee cords aren't affected by sea salt or moisture like some hooks are. So there is no need to worry about losing the hooks or replacing rusty hooks.

Warning Light

Be careful when handling bungee cords. Keep them high enough so that children don't try to play with them. The elasticity that they possess can fling a cord across the room or into an eye.

Regular bungee cords are also good for securing items. If you lean your ladder against the wall, put a screw or a hook on each side of it. String the bungee across the hooks to keep the ladder from sliding to the floor or falling forward. You can use this for a number of tools and equipment that hang from the wall with screws or nails.

This bungee keeps the ladder from falling into the garage.

Photo by Theresa Russell

Alligator Board

This is a fancy pegboard. It comes in a variety of colors and finishes and is easy to install. The different color options make this a way to add some flair to your garage wall. You can use the different color boards for organizing different types of tools.

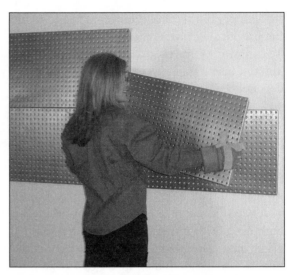

It's easy to install the Alligator Board.

Photo by Alligator Board

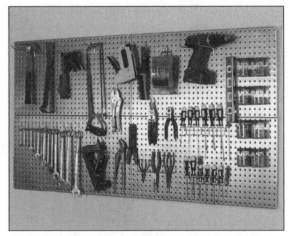

You just need a small space for this board.

Photo by Alligator Board

The Alligator Board is the fancy cousin of the ordinary pegboard. Because it is made from perforated metal, it is more durable. With this material, you have no worries about scraping the board itself or having scratched out sections like you could with the regular pressed pegboard.

Its shiny good looks will add a bit of sparkle to your garage. This is installed just like any other type of pegboard. Their choice of colors lets you customize the look of your garage. If you just need a short strip for hanging tools, they have that, too.

Rail Systems

The rail systems have nothing to do with trains. The concept is based on installing long rails at a certain distance apart.

This system is fluid and easy to change around the configuration.

Photo by Schulte

The main rail is installed vertically on the wall and any number of "uprights," slotted metal rails, can be added. A variety of accessories fits into these slots. Ventilated shelves, baskets, cabinets, and more make it easy for you to get your stuff off the floor. The manufacturers claim that you do not have to screw this system into studs (because it comes with spiraled anchors). We personally prefer the extra strength that studs offer.

Slat Walls

Next time you are in a department store, take a look at the walls. You might see that they are covered with slatted boards. There are shelves, hangers, and racks attached to these boards. No screws or nails are required after the slats have been installed.

The slat wall is attractive.

Photo by Schulte

This same type of product is becoming popular for garages. You have to install it, but installation is pretty straightforward for most any type of garage. You can cover an entire wall or every wall in your garage with slat boards. You could just use a few sections to take care of a smaller number of hanging things. Installation on concrete block walls can be accomplished using one of the techniques described in the previous section on challenging installations.

Floor It

You've heard it a thousand times already, but we'll say it again: if you can keep stuff off the floor, do it. Certain things like the roll-around tool chests do stay on the floor, but the wheels keep the entire cart from being on the floor. One reason to keep things off the floor is because those things take up precious space. Another reason is that they can interfere with the traffic pattern or be another obstruction to negotiation. Sometimes the floor can be a damp spot, and the water might seep into your containers.

Stackable Systems

Plan on using a waterproof material for anything that will be on the floor. Recycling bins are typically put on the floor, but there are ways to keep them off the floor. One way is with the stackable shelving systems available.

These shelves come apart and can be rearranged providing you with different levels of stacking space.

Photo by Theresa Russell

Other things that go on the floor are free-standing products. Most of this doesn't totally touch the floor. There is a slight clearance to keep them off the floor.

Think about storage crates like you used in the dorm. Some are made with wire so that you can easily see what is in them. There are all different sizes of covered containers. These stack easily, too.

The Rest

You most likely will keep your larger equipment on the floor. The lawn mower, lawn tractor, and snow blower are too heavy to hang on the wall. There are raised platforms that can get these out of the way.

Ceilings

Look up for more storage above your head. As long as you have a higher ceiling in your garage, it could be another option for storing things. You already know about hooks that you can hang up in the joists. A few more systems take a bit more effort to install, but are still relatively easy to do.

Racks

Yes, some racks can be attached to the joists or the ceiling. They hang down, so be sure you have plenty of clearance.

Drive It Home

Measure the thickness, width, and length of your ceiling joists. Go online, go to your local library, or go to your local building department and find a span table. Find your joist dimensions and see whether they are adequate for the span in your garage. Also check to see whether they are within the allowable dimensions for carrying the live load of what you want to hang from them. If you have any doubts or questions, ask at your local building department.

Be sure that the joists are strong enough to support the weight. They are excellent for storing odd-shaped or little-used items.

Using this space will keep your floor clear. This is a great place to store things if you have a concrete garage.

Ceiling racks free up floor space.

Photo by Hyloft

It isn't quite the ceiling, but it is up there. Inventors come up with new ideas all the time. The Addahook uses the rails of the garage door as a place to find extra storage. The hook fastens into the rails.

The Addahook takes advantage of the garage door rail.

Photo by Addahook

There are definite weight limits for using this. Therefore, be really certain that whatever you hang won't whack you in the head when you get out of your car.

Pulleys

A pulley system is an excellent way to get those big or odd-size items out of the way. You can put your cartop carrier, bicycles, kayaks, or canoes up near the ceiling with the help of the pulley.

Pulleys make lifting heavy objects simple.

Photo by GarageTek

Confirm that your joists are up to code. If they are underbuilt or underspaced, you shouldn't attach anything to them. Heavy items may cause excessive stress. This stress could make the joists sag, which can cause the roof to sag. Our house with an attached garage had the garage door track mounted on inadequate ceiling joists. These joists cracked and sagged because of this. The previous owner also had added a ceiling, which caused even more problems. We had to do some structural reinforcements to correct the problem.

Warning Light

Always be sure that the structural components of your garage are up to code and up to the duty that you want them to perform.

Remember those science lessons in grade school about how the pulley saves work? This is exactly why the pulley is a great option. It saves your back and is especially helpful if you have problems lifting. It also saves you from climbing up the ladder and trying to hold on to something cumbersome. Best of all, it gets things off the floor and out of the way.

Between the Joists

Look at all that wasted space between the joists. Don't see it? Then you must have a finished garage. In that case, you don't need to read this section. The advantage of this space is that it doesn't necessarily invade the rest of your overhead garage space.

This space has potential, too.

Photo by Theresa Russell

This spot lends itself well to putting those extra pieces of lumber or PVC pipes. If you happen to have cross-bracing in place, you may be limited as to what you can store in between the joists.

Drive It Home

The typical measurement of the joist space is from 5 to 11 inches high, 14.5 to 22.5 inches wide, and as long as the distance between cross-bracing and the walls.

Think about storing seasonal items up here. Those fishing poles might fit rather nicely. The flags you hang in the summer would fit up here nicely, too.

It bears repeating that your joists and garage ceiling need to be structurally sound and adequately sized before hanging anything from them.

Here are a few tips for a quick visual overview that will show obvious problems. If you are unsure about the structural integrity of your garage, call a structural engineer, architect, or code inspector. Most home inspection services that focus on real estate do *not* have this knowledge.

Above the Rafters

Do you have space above the joists? Is it easily accessible? Can you access if from a second-story room?

If you have space above the garage, you have even more options for storing things. The first thing you will need is something to lay across the joists. If it is already floored, you are in luck. If it isn't floored, you have a few options for laying a flat surface up there. Now keep in mind that there are some objects that might easily fit perpendicularly to the joists. A floor isn't absolutely necessary in that case. Think about how you will get up to that space. Is a ladder adequate for accessing that space? Is there a stairway that pulls down to access the space? If you just want to add flooring over part or all of the space, keep reading.

The extra space in the attic is useful for seasonal storage.

Photo by Rand Ruland

Before you take any sheathing up to the attic space, decide how much maneuvering space you have up there. If your roof has a shallow pitch, you may not have much room at all to get your flooring up there. If you have knee walls, you may have a limited amount of usable space. Trusses could totally eliminate the usable space you have above the ceiling.

Warning Light

Be very careful about walking on any surface that may already be lying across the joists. Especially in an older attic space, it is quite possible that the surface is not well supported and that you could fall through. If there is no flooring, you could lose your footing if you are standing on the joists and fall through the drywall on the ceiling below or just fall between the joists.

If you decide your attic space has storage potential, follow these steps for installing an attic space floor:

1. To determine the carrying capacity of your joists, first measure the thickness, width, and length of your ceiling joists. Go online, go to your local library, or go to your local building department and find a span table. Find your joist dimensions (thickness, width, and length) in the span table and see whether they are adequate for the span in your garage. Also check to see whether they are within the allowable dimensions for carrying the live load of what you want to store on them. If you have any doubts or questions, ask at the building department.

2. Determine the maximum size of boards or sheets you can easily get into the attic space. Can you get a full 4'×8' sheet of plywood into the space? Half a sheet? Maybe you need to consider 1'×8' or 1'×10' boards. Do you have narrow stairs to negotiate? Can you simply push the material up in between the joists?

3. Calculate the amount of floor space you can efficiently use in the attic. When the distance between the floor and the roof is less than 2 feet, it becomes more difficult to access items stored there, especially if other things are piled in front. Measure a reasonable rectangle that can be covered by your flooring. If you are using 4'×8' sheets, consider floor dimensions that require minimal cutting and waste of those sheets.

4. Purchase enough flooring material to cover that space.

5. Cut the boards to appropriate lengths or cut the sheets to a size that you can physically get into the space easily and safely.

6. If your joist spacing is 16 inches on center, use at least a ¹/₂" thick board or sheet of flooring.

7. If your space is 24 inches on center, use a ³/₄" thick sheet or board for flooring.

8. If there is no insulation between the joists and you plan to eventually heat the garage, you may want to improve the energy efficiency. If you already have heat or air, now is the time to install insulation before installing the floor. Make sure that you do not block any vents or ventilation areas, such as perforated soffits, when installing your insulation.

9. Install the flooring using 2" drywall screws. I prefer screws to nails because they are more easily removed and provide a stronger attachment.

10. Make your boards and sheets meet *only* on the joists. End the board or sheet on a joist, too.

Bring It All Back

Finally, you have found the systems that will make your garage look great. Everything has its own spot. Bring everything back into the garage and put it in its place.

Did you overlook anything? Did you forget about something you stored somewhere else? If so, look at your design plan and see where you can fit it in. If there isn't a place, you may have to start from scratch or find another place to store whatever you had forgotten about.

This is a nicely organized garage.

Photo by Gladiator

When you put your items in a container, be sure to immediately label the container. If you are storing a lot of things, label it with a number or letter. Take an inventory of everything you put in there. You could store that list inside the box, or better yet, type up a sheet on the computer and save it. If you need to know what is in container A, you simply go to your computer and look it up. If you are storing a bunch of similar items, it is a more simple matter. Just mark the container tools, gardening, seasonal, or whatever. If you have more than one box of any category, it is helpful to have a list of what is in there, or use subcategories to identify it. If you have two boxes of tools, you could label them "drywall tools" and "auto repair tools." Use whatever system works best for you, but do have a system.

The Least You Need to Know

- Using the walls and ceilings makes good organizational sense.
- New products solve your storage needs.
- Attaching anything to concrete requires extra effort, tools, and special techniques.
- Assess your structure and be sure that it is up to the task.
- Floor your attic for extra storage space.
- Mark your containers to quickly find your things.

In This Chapter

- ◆ Equipping your garage to accommodate your life-style

- ◆ Finding a place for everything

- ◆ Making it work for you

- ◆ Dedicating spaces for specific uses

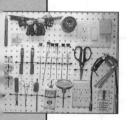  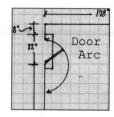   

11

The Practical Garage

You may have your kid's outdoor toys, sports equipment, or your pet's cage and supplies stored in your garage. Maybe you are a gardener and have your soil, pots, and seeds out there. Maybe you're a car fanatic with your automotive supplies. So what is practical for your situation? What are the basics every garage needs?

Practical means different things to different people. For some, it means having the latest and greatest tool, whether you even have any intention of using it or not. For others, it means having a space for keeping the contents in order and making the items easily accessible. If you want to have a few things to make your garage practical, keep reading.

Automotive Tools and Accessories

If you are responsible for the maintenance of your car or enjoy making automotive repairs, you might want to keep a few products in your garage for that purpose.

Keeping the Car Clean

The most basic thing a car owner can do to take care of the car is to keep it clean. Keeping all your supplies in one spot can make the job easier.

Keep all your cleaning products and supplies in a bucket. You can store your cleaners, sponges, brushes, and wax in one spot and keep it on a shelf, hang it from a hook, or place it in a convenient place on the floor. That way, when you need to wash the car, you have no excuse. Everything is together.

A couple of other items help when it comes to cleaning the car:

◆ A hose is something you can't wash the car without. You can hang it on a hook near your supply bucket so that it is close at hand.

◆ A Shop Vac or small handheld vacuum can make it easy to get the crumbs and chunks up off the car floor. Shop vacuums come in all different strengths and sizes. For the car, you need just the standard tools and some good suction. Many of these vacuums have wet and dry capabilities. That means you can clean any spills in the car with the same piece of equipment that you are using to suck up the other dirt. Some vacs are designed more for heavy-duty work and have extra features that make their use in the workshop practical. You can store them in a cabinet or underneath the workbench.

◆ A bucket is perfect for keeping everything from sponges to cleaners. You can put the bucket on a shelf, hang it from a hook, or put it in a convenient place on the floor.

Drive It Home

Use plastic storage bins to keep your car organized. Label bins clearly. Use over-the-visor holders for CDs and, if you have kids, make use of organizers that hang over the backs of the front seats so the kids have easy access to the items that keep them occupied in the car and you can easily see what items need replenishing. Collapsible soft-sided bins are available for the backs of vans and SUVs that will contain shopping and grocery bags and prevent them from spilling their contents.

This is a simple solution for keeping everything for cleaning the car.

Photo by Theresa Russell

Regular Maintenance

Those who change the oil or spark plugs or do other auto maintenance have a whole other list of items to keep on hand. You should start by keeping some replacement parts such as oil filters, spark plugs, oil, and antifreeze.

Warning Light

Antifreeze is composed of a type of glycol, usually ethylene glycol, which is poisonous to both animals and people. Don't ever leave it out where kids and pets can get to it. If you spill it, clean it immediately so that your pet doesn't have a chance to try to lick it up. If ingested, notify a physician or poison control center immediately.

You also will need some tools for your auto maintenance, including oil filter wrenches, spark plug wrenches, oil pans, and whatever else you would need. In some areas, a heater for diesel engines is handy.

Drive It Home

Properly dispose of used oil. Many commercial oil-change companies and auto parts stores recycle oil for no charge. Simply take your old oil to them. Your community recycling center may also take used oil. I have found the plastic containers that I buy cat litter in are convenient for dropping off used oil.

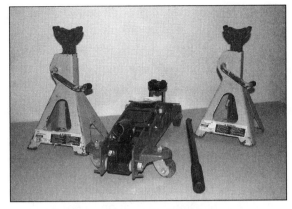

These are convenient for lifting the car.
Photo by Theresa Russell

Heavier Maintenance Work

If you do serious automotive work, you probably own a set of ramps, a jack, jack stands, and maybe even a creeper that rolls under the car. These accessories can take up quite a bit of space in the garage. Think about ways to store them as efficiently as possible. You may want to visit your local auto parts store to see what type of storage cabinets are available for automotive equipment. The creeper can slide under a bench or hang on a door.

Warning Light

When you put your car up on ramps, put some type of effective blocks behind the wheels still on the floor. If you use a jack, always use wheel blocks and jack stands. Do not let children play around the vehicle.

If you are thinking of doing bodywork in your garage, you have extra-special needs, especially for setting up a paint booth and for ventilation. This will necessitate meeting additional safety requirements. Your local building code office should be able to provide you with the information you need or be able to direct you to where you can find it.

Diehard auto mechanics might dream of having a lift in their garage. These can transform your garage into a professional workspace. Not only will a four-post lift make certain repairs much easier, you can also store two cars in the space that you previously only stored one. Installing a lift or modifying your garage to efficiently handle auto body work and painting will require a professional evaluation to ensure that the installation and subsequent use will be safe.

Drive It Home

Climate control in a garage not only makes you more comfortable, it also protects anything stored in the garage from the effects of moisture and temperature extremes. Even without a complete HVAC system, your belongings are better off in the garage than outside. In damp conditions, older cars, especially, can fail to start because of a wet ignition.

Yard and Garden Tools

Maintaining your lawn and garden requires many special tools. If you are a serious gardener, you may need special containers for your plants, wheelbarrows, and other products. Some of the largest machinery in the garage is for lawn and yard care.

Lawn mowers, snow blowers, and rototillers all take up a lot of real estate in the garage. If you find that they are taking over the garage, think about putting a shed or other dedicated area outside for them. Obviously, if you have enough room for them, just be sure that they

are out of the traffic pattern. Think about which tools are used most often in which season. Provide an area for frequently used equipment. The rototiller might occupy it in the spring, the lawn mower in the summer, the leaf blower in the fall and the snow blower in the winter. If you are constantly stubbing your toes on one of these pieces of equipment, think of a better way to store them (or perhaps give them their own dedicated storage building).

Larger garden tools fit nicely on the wall.

Photo by Schulte

A separate shed for large items is practical.

Photo by Theresa Russell

Other useful implements gardeners use include weed whackers, a variety of rakes, shovels, small tools, hoes, scythes, watering cans, and hoses. Transplanting, seeding, and other garden duties can be done in a space devoted just to the pursuit of this passion.

A potting bench is ideal for the avid gardener. Propagating roses in the comfort of your garage beats doing it in the sun. When your passion for gardening starts to infringe on other areas of the garage, it is time to think about your own potting shed where you can work undistracted by the other spaces in your garage.

If you want to stay in the garage, be creative with how you store your tools. Make them part of the décor if necessary.

Consider a dedicated area for gardening needs.

Photo by GarageTek

Your lawn carts and tracker need to be easily accessible through most of the year. Clippers and pruners and other tools should always be easy to reach. The bags that fertilizer, topsoil, and seeds come in usually suffice for getting it home from the store, but soon after seem to tear and leak. Consider transferring those loose products to some large storage containers, which can be stacked and more easily arranged than partially full bags.

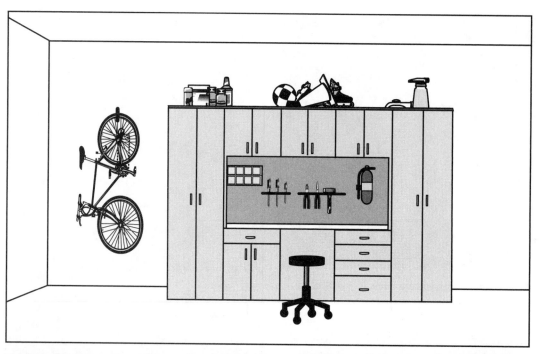

An example of a sketch and the realized layout.

Photos by ClosetMaid

You probably have water outside the garage, but wouldn't a sink in the garage be a real help? If this is something that you would like to consider adding, read more about what's involved in Chapter 16.

Sports Equipment

Most people have some sort of sporting equipment. Skiing, snowboarding, snowshoeing, and tobogganing are all popular winter sports. The equipment isn't the smallest or most regular shape, so it poses a storage problem. Not only is it necessary to find a space for it, but these things are often so oddly shaped that they leave strangely shaped areas in their wake.

These skis are out of the path of travel.

Photo by GarageTek

Specialty racks are made for skis, boots, and poles. Some of them rest on the floor; others can be put up on the wall or hung from the ceiling. This is the type of equipment that you want to have readily available in season, but don't need in such a prominent place off-season. Maybe the poles and ski boots can be switched with hiking sticks and hiking boots in the summer. If you have the old-style snowshoes, you can easily put them on the wall. They are ready-made décor items for any garage wall. Newer snowshoes have cleats on the bottom, so an alternate storage solution will work better. These also can be stored in an out-of-the-way place in the off-season. They often come with a storage pouch, which can be hung on any hook or placed on a shelf.

Warning Light

Protruding blades from sleds, skis, and ice skates are hazardous, and the crampons on snowshoes can inflict serious damage to the skin. Be sure that sharp parts of equipment are protected or turned so that grabbing the bag storing them doesn't result in injury. Use covers on blades and any sharp parts.

Sleds and toboggans can go above the joists or hang on the wall. Remember to keep anything with blades placed in a way that avoids potential injury.

Baskets are a popular way to hold skates and hockey equipment. No worries about running around finding everything for practice.

If you participate in a sport that requires changing shoes, consider putting a small bench in the garage for this purpose. Be clever and use a strong storage container as a combination storage/changing bench. It can serve as a practical place for changing boots, putting on kneepads, or getting the kids ready to play in the snow, too.

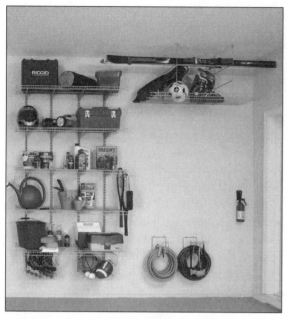

This system keeps skiing equipment out of the way.

Photo by ClosetMaid

Baskets are a handy way for storing odd-shaped things.

Photo by Schulte

Warm-weather sports equipment includes inline skates, bicycles, soccer nets and balls, canoes, kayaks, and boats, camping equipment, and more. The difficulty of storing items in this category is size and shape are not consistent. A fishing boat takes up a bit more space than a soccer ball. The good news is product manufacturers have taken this all into account and have created some interesting solutions for storing these sports accessories.

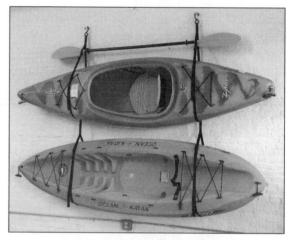

This simple system gets kayaks off the floor.

Photo by Riverside

Pulleys make lifting heavier equipment easier and make it possible to get it out of the way. Hooking devices keep bikes out of the way. Adding straps around a kayak is a simple way to attach that to a few hooks. Walls work as well for these objects.

Photo by GarageTek

Photo by Schulte

There are several ways to store a bicycle.

Photo by GarageTek

Although the golf bag is an efficient storage space for golfing equipment, the bag itself can be moved off the floor. This keeps it from falling into the path of parking cars. Several products are made specifically for golf bags. But storage lockers or large cabinets also work well.

Camping gear takes up a lot of space. Follow manufacturers' recommendations for storing accessories. Tents often come with storage bags. Place these on shelves or in bins with other camping equipment.

Pay particular attention to anything that uses fuel. Do not put the fuel into a storage bin with the rest of your camping equipment. Store it as you would any other hazardous product.

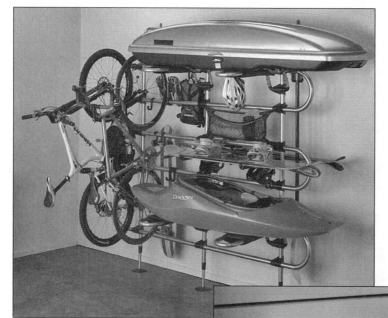

This rack stores a variety of equipment.

Photo by Yakima

This system keeps bags and shoes at the ready.

Photo by Schulte

Simple shelves are excellent for camping gear.

Photo by Schulte

Toys

If you have children or grandchildren, you probably have toys. If you still have toys and the kids are long gone, go back to Chapter 6 and clear things out.

Toys come in assorted shapes and sizes. Wagons, riding toys, t-ball, bikes, and trampolines all need a home.

Things such as trampolines and kiddie pools can stay outside during swimming season but need an inside spot the rest of the year.

Kids' toys should be neatly organized.

Photo by Hyloft

It seems that toys especially have a tendency to get in the way. Start getting your children into the habit of putting away their toys in the spot that you have designated. Large cubbyhole storage units are ideal. These are often used in kindergarten and grade schools. Everything is easily visible, and there are no drawers or doors to injure little hands.

Baskets and bins are ideal for storing those odd-shaped things. Be sure to keep things at a comfortable kid level so that the kids can be responsible for retrieving and storing their own toys.

Loose Change

Kids love to write and draw on chalkboards or whiteboards. If you have a section of blank wall space in the garage, consider hanging a piece of inexpensive whiteboard and getting the kids some dry erase markers. 4'×8' sheets of plain white bathroom panels, called thrifty white, sell for about $10 and make good whiteboards. The sheets cut easily and can be cheaply replaced. Another option is to hang a piece of hardboard and paint it with chalkboard paint, which is available at any paint supply store.

Pets and Supplies

You might have a pet door that leads into the garage from your house. Fido's dish or Kitty's litter box could reside in the garage. If their food is stored there, it should be kept so that it doesn't attract rodents or insects. A large sealed container works well for this purpose. Things such as animal carriers could easily fit in the rafters or on shelves. Some dogs have a special cage in the garage where they stay for part of the day.

Seasonal

Some of the items in your garage get used for just part of the year or for just a few weeks. Some people enjoy decorating the interior and exterior of their homes to coordinate with the holidays. Our neighbors do something significant for every holiday and every season, even when there isn't a major "decorating" holiday. To easily access these decorations, it means keeping them and properly locating them in an accessible space that allows for easy rotation if there is more than one container for these decorations.

Drive It Home

Before storing seasonal items, be sure they are in good operating condition. Don't put burned-out lights away for the year. If something can be repaired, do it now. If it is beyond repair, pitch it.

Other seasonal items include sleds, pools, toboggans, and snow shovels. If there is adequate space to store them year-round, that is not a problem. But if space is at a premium, it is a good idea to move the unused and unnecessary things to an out-of-the-way place. Concentrate on keeping items for current use in a more accessible spot.

Loose Change

Often at the time when you are storing your seasonal goods, the stores are getting rid of their seasonal items at a greatly reduced cost. This is the ideal time to replace broken or worn items at a reduced cost.

Don't forget to bring in your patio, porch, and lawn furniture and accessories. Clean everything before you store it. Remember, chairs are often stackable, and tables come apart. If any of this outdoor furniture takes up too much space in the garage, either cover it or consider getting an outdoor shed for storage.

Hazardous Products

It may sound odd that a well-equipped garage would have some hazardous products. Just think about what you use in the course of the year. Paint, paint thinner, propane, polyurethane, fertilizer, cleaners, bleach, and other solvents often get stored in the garage. Read the labels for tips on storage and disposal. Don't keep those things in the garage when you have finished using them. Store poisons out of the reach of children, locking them in a cabinet if necessary.

Warning Light

When my children were growing up, they often accompanied me to job-sites. I removed blades from saws and bits from drills when transporting them or when I was finished using them. Whenever possible, I used cases to store the power hand tools. It took a little effort and time, but the worst that happened to those curious little hands were nicks and small scratches.

Besides chemically hazardous products, some tools could be especially dangerous in young hands. Don't leave power tools lying around or on the workbench when not in use, and certainly don't leave them plugged in. It wouldn't be a pretty sight if one of the kids decided to play with a planer, band saw, or any other tool. Some tools have safety locks on them to prevent this. Be sure that the lock is on. Put the tools away in a cabinet when you are done with them. If you have such tools, keep on eye on the kids if they are in the garage.

Appliances and Fixtures

The deep freezer, the beer refrigerator, or the washer and dryer are often placed in the garage. Many people simply move the old appliances into the garage when they get new ones in the house. If the garage isn't climate-controlled, this can wreak havoc on the appliances.

The dampness of the garage can quickly damage the surface of the appliances. Not surprisingly, some newer models of appliances are made specifically for the garage.

If you have plumbing in the garage and have some space, consider putting the laundry in the garage. Stackable washers and dryers make good use of vertical space.

Some models are made specifically for garages.

Photo by Gladiator

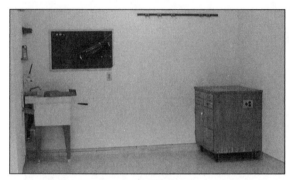

This laundry sink is convenient for dealing with messy jobs.

Photo by Erik Russell

A sink is convenient for cleaning up after working on the car or in the garden. A larger tub-style sink is ideal for cleaning large items, soaking laundry, or giving a large pet a bath.

Ambience

For some people a bit of background entertainment is a plus, especially for those who spend long hours in their garages. Televisions, music systems, and computers enhance the overall experience. Watching a favorite show or listening to music can make washing the car or sorting through tools a more pleasant experience.

Industrial-grade phones are perfect for those who want a dedicated telephone line in the garage rather than just a cell phone.

The type of ambience you create in your garage is one of personal preference.

Special Events

If you host the weekly bridge club or poker game, a space in the garage keeps guests away from your family who might be distracted by the rabble-rousing that goes on when people get together.

Ping-Pong tables work well in garage spaces, as do other bar-type games such as darts, bumper pool, and even regular pool if you have the space. Ping-Pong tables often come in folding models. Card tables, banquet tables, or folding chairs can be stored away quickly and easily.

Safety

What kinds of safety features should you have in your garage? How about childproof locks on cabinets? A safe garage door and opener are a must. A touchpad for keyless entry is not only convenient, it also secures an entry to your home. If your home has a security system, make sure that all garage windows and doors are covered by it. Smoke detectors, carbon monoxide detectors, and other warning devices are all appropriate. Lots of utility light and adequate overhead lighting are important, too.

The Least You Need to Know

- ◆ Resist the urge to fill every bit of space with stuff.
- ◆ Keep the appropriate tools you need for your tasks and activities stored and accessible.
- ◆ Store sports equipment and toys safely and out of the way.
- ◆ Move large items that require too much space to another area or dedicated shed.
- ◆ Keep your children and yourself safe by properly storing hazardous materials and potentially dangerous items.
- ◆ Enjoy the functionality of your practical garage.

In This Chapter

- ◆ Creating your workspace
- ◆ Finding the right workbench
- ◆ Building your own workbench
- ◆ Choosing tools and safety equipment

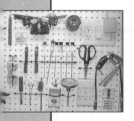  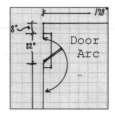   

12

Home Maintenance Workshop

More and more homeowners, both men and women, are assuming greater responsibility for home maintenance and improvement projects. If you want to get more involved in your home maintenance and improvement projects, the first thing you need is a workspace. This is where you can store your tools, organize your hardware and maintenance supplies, and safely and efficiently work on projects. Creating this workspace requires some time, effort, and thought.

Although every home should have a home maintenance workshop, the term *workshop* is relative. Your workshop could be a simple pegboard or a toolbox. Another home workshop may include a large workbench and tool cabinets fully stocked with all sorts of hammers, screwdrivers, wrenches, and specialty tools. Let's consider these options and some in between to help you find the solution you need.

The Workspace

As you progressed through the design and planning phases of the previous chapters, you should have assigned some space to be dedicated to your home maintenance workshop. Perhaps it was a section of pegboard for hanging tools and storing supplies. Maybe it was space in a cabinet for a toolbox containing essential tools and assorted hardware.

The advantages of a toolbox are many. It is easy to store and easy to move. You can take it right to the site where you are making a repair or assembling a new purchase. It does have a limited capacity for tools and it cannot hold larger tools.

The portable workbench is another option to consider. It provides a small but adequate work surface. It is usually adjustable and provides some storage for tools. Many models are foldable or collapsible. This means they can be stored away or made into smaller, more compact units when they are not in use. Like the toolbox, these are easy to move to the jobsite.

Portable workstations can be found at most home improvement centers. You can choose from a variety of styles, such as a foldable work-table or a movable bench on heavy-duty casters.

A portable workbench can go where it is needed with handy access to tools, and it can be moved out of the way when no longer needed.

Photo by Coleman

The final option to consider is the stationary workbench. It should have the capacity to handle all your jobs. With this option, all work must be brought to the workbench. This type of workbench takes up more room, but provides more storage space for tools and supplies and is more sturdy and steady.

Warning Light _____

Unless you make a strong effort to prevent it, the workbench can become disorganized. The large flat surface can become a catchall for all sorts of objects. Clear it off when you finish each project and don't be tempted to toss things there.

You can purchase ready-to-go stationary benches or kits requiring some assembly. Some hardware kits provide all the brackets, braces, and fasteners for your workbench. You just provide the lumber. You also could build one from scratch. We give you instructions for a simple do-it-yourself workbench in the next section.

A stationary workbench not only provides a solid surface to work on, but also provides significant storage area.

Photo by Gladiator

Powering Your Workbench

Do you have adequate electrical service in your work area? Ideally, you should have outlets located about 3 feet apart along the wall, preferably above the workbench. You want to minimize the use and number of extension cords around your work area.

$ Loose Change

You may be able to use a multiple-outlet power strip at your workbench. Some plug into an existing outlet and can be mounted on a wall. This could save you the trouble and expense of rewiring. Some portable workbenches even come with power strips built into them.

There should be individual, dedicated service for any large power equipment, such as an air compressor. All circuits in a garage should be protected with ground fault interruption to prevent shock.

Drive It Home

Find the circuit breaker controlling the garage outlets in your breaker panel and make sure it is 20 amps and not already serving multiple other areas. Otherwise, you may be tripping the breaker when using a couple of tools simultaneously.

In case you need to modify or add to your existing circuits, we provide some instructions in Chapter 16. You may, however, feel more comfortable having an electrician upgrade your electrical service. While that's happening, you may want to evaluate the lighting in your workshop and improve the workspace lighting.

This breaker box has 20-amp breakers for receptacle circuits and 15-amp breakers for light circuits.

Photo by Robert Russell

Warning Light

When you are done with your tools, don't leave them plugged in. I have had older tools or ones with faulty switches that started sparking or creating problems when plugged in, but not in use. Better yet, when you are done with your tools, put them away.

Shedding Some Light

Do you have adequate lighting? Can you see those nails on the workbench, or are you essentially working in the dark? Make sure your lights are on a separate circuit from the outlets so that you won't lose the lights when a breaker trips while using a power tool. Fluorescent overhead lights are durable, energy efficient, and inexpensive. Position them so that shadows are minimized when you are working at the bench. Portable clip-on lights are handy to have, too, to provide illumination to specific areas. For more information on lighting, check out Chapter 16.

This inexpensive light is easy to attach almost anywhere.

Photo by Theresa Russell

Keeping the Air Comfortable

How about ventilation? Depending on what you are doing in your work area, you might create enough dust particles and heat to make the surrounding atmosphere unpleasant. There are several ways to set up a ventilation system. Opening windows and doors may be adequate. You also can set up fans to draw fresh air from the outside and expel stale, dust-laden air from the inside. If you are considering doing auto bodywork or doing woodworking requiring stains and finishes with potent fumes, you might consider a heavy-duty exhaust system.

A reversible window fan can be handy for expelling dust as well as keeping cool.

Photo by Nathan Russell

You may want to consider one of those twin-fan combinations for windows. These pull in air on one side and expel it on the other. Previous owners at one of our houses left a heavy-duty reversible window fan. It is quite large and has multiple speeds that work in both directions. This is one of the few useful things left in the house, and it has been perfect for expelling dust and odors from the house.

Drive It Home

Many newer tools have built-in dust-collection ports. These can be attached to a shop vacuum and run simultaneously with the tool. It keeps the air cleaner and saves you from having to clean up afterward.

Dust-collection systems can be set up for individual tools or a whole shop if your projects produce a lot of dust.

A vacuum running while using the saw collects most of the dust created when cutting.

Photo by Theresa Russell

A complete climate-control system with air filtration also can be installed, although this could be costly. Because of potentially hazardous vapors or dust and to prevent the spread or feeding of a fire, the HVAC system in a garage should be separate from the house. A heating and cooling system also will protect your tools and equipment from rust, mold, and the effects of climate change. We talk more about HVAC systems and ventilation in Chapter 16.

Build a Workbench

Your workbench, whether portable or stationary, is the most important part of your workshop. You want a solid surface that won't wobble or move around while you are working on a project. It needs to be strong enough to hold heavy objects and large enough to accommodate sizable projects. The top surface should be at a comfortable working height. Thirty-six inches off the floor is a standard height. My taller friends have extended the legs on commercially produced models or have built their

own with a height of as much as 40 inches. My shorter friends have built workbenches with tops as low as 30 inches.

> **$ Loose Change**
>
> If you are on a tight budget, consider some alternatives for modifying something into a workbench. Perhaps you could extend the legs on a sturdy old table. My daughter's workplace gets some very sturdy shipping crates that could easily be modified. I've used a couple of clean 55-gallon drums with a plywood top. Just be sure it will handle the pounding and related efforts of your projects.

This could be a future workbench.

Photo by Robert Russell

We are now going to discuss building a utility workbench that can be assembled in an afternoon. We will use inexpensive, common building materials that can be found at any home improvement center. Many of these centers will cut the material for you at a minimal or no charge. You need to purchase six 2×4s and one 4'×8' sheet of ¾" thick *plywood*, *OSB*, or *MDF.*

Definitions

Plywood is the first engineered wood product constructed of gluing thin sheets or veneers of wood with the grain running at right angles.

OSB, oriented strand board, is constructed by gluing rectangular strands of hardwood/softwood laid up in layers at right angles to each other.

MDF, medium-density fiberboard, is a type of hardboard produced by gluing uniformly processed wood fibers under heat and pressure.

The face and edge of plywood, OSB, and MDF.

Photo by Theresa Russell

These materials will not make a fine piece of furniture. They will make a useful, abusable, renewable work horse. We chose MDF for our top and shelf and 2×4 softwood lumber for the frame. The MDF is inexpensive, flat, and straight, and cuts easily enough with carbide-tipped tools.

As you work on this surface, you can cut, dent, hammer, drill, and saw into it, and not worry about it or damaging your tools. When it gets really worn, unscrew it and replace it or fasten another top right over it.

Materials List:

- (6) 2"×4"s
- (8) 21" cross braces
- (2) 48" shelf frames
- (2) 64" top frames
- (4) 35" legs (increase or decrease the length to your needs)
- $^3/_4$" sheet goods
- 24"×48" shelf
- 24"×64" top
- Approximately 50 3" drywall screws
- Approximately 30 2" drywall screws

Tools Needed:

- Pencil
- Tape measure
- Square
- Saw (circular, miter, or hand to cut 2×4s)
- Drill with #2 Phillips bit and $^5/_{32}$" wood bit

It will be helpful to read through the directions and study the pictures before attempting to build the workbench. You will gain some insight into why certain holes are drilled where and why certain pieces are aligned in relation to others.

Warning Light

Correct safety precautions should always be taken when cutting or sanding engineered wood products. The glues and resins may cause irritation to the eyes and lungs. Proper ventilation is required when working with it, and masks and goggles should always be used when cutting or sanding it with power tools.

The cutting edges of regular steel tools will dull quickly because of the amount of glue and resin contained in these products. Carbide-tipped tools are recommended.

We've gathered our tools.

Photo by Theresa Russell

Back from the home improvement center with our supplies.

Photo by Theresa Russell

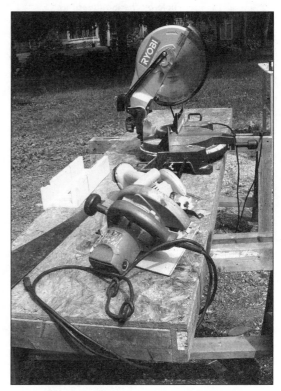

Any one of these can be used to cut 2×4s.

Photo by Theresa Russell

Mark and cut the 2×4s as shown.

Photo by Theresa Russell

This is what you should end up with. From left to right, the top frames, the shelf frames, the legs, and the cross braces.

Photo by Theresa Russell

Set the two top frame pieces next to each other and mark where the cross braces will be attached as shown. Each of the narrow spaces is 1½" wide to match the actual width of the cross brace. Draw an X in the 1½" space where the cross brace goes.

Photo by Theresa Russell

Do the same thing to the shelf frames.

Photo by Theresa Russell

Drill two $^5/_{32}$" clearance holes $^3/_4$" from the edge as shown in each of the cross brace spaces that were marked with an X.

Photo by Theresa Russell

Assemble the top frame using 3" drywall screws.

Photo by Theresa Russell

Assemble the shelf frame using 3" drywall screws.

Photo by Theresa Russell

The completed frames.

Photo by Theresa Russell

Place the top frame on the top, make sure the edges are flush and draw an outline around the 2×4s.

Photo by Theresa Russell

Drill $^5/_{32}$" clearance holes centered in the $1^1/_2$" spaces of the outline you drew. For the top, place five holes evenly spaced along the long sides and one hole in the middle for each cross brace. For the shelf, place three holes evenly spaced along the long sides, starting 8 inches from the ends, and one hole in the middle for each of the three cross braces.

Photo by Theresa Russell

Do the same thing with the shelf and the shelf frame.

Photo by Theresa Russell

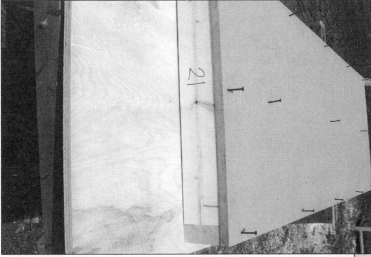

Turn the top over onto the top frame, align the edges, and fasten with 2" drywall screws.

Photo by Theresa Russell

Mark each leg 4 inches from one end for positioning the shelf.

Photo by Theresa Russell

Turn the top assembly over and drill three $^5/_{32}$" clearance holes for attaching each leg, as shown at the inside cross braces.

Photo by Theresa Russell

Place a leg in each inside cross brace corner with the 4" mark up and outside. Attach each leg with three 3" drywall screws. Use a square to make sure the legs are perpendicular to the top.

Photo by Theresa Russell

On the long side of the shelf frame, drill two $5/32$" clearance holes at each end 4 inches from the end and $3/4$ inches from the edge. Then drill one $5/32$" clearance hole at each end centered $2 3/4$ inches from the end.

Photo by Theresa Russell

Carefully rotate the assembly onto its side and place the shelf frame over the legs. Position the shelf so the shelf will be above the 4" mark you previously made. Attach the shelf frame to a leg at each corner with three 3" drywall screws through the clearance holes you just drilled.

Photo by Theresa Russell

Carefully turn the bench upright.

Photo by Theresa Russell

Cut a $5 1/8$" by $3 1/8$" notch from each corner of the shelf as shown. These will allow room for the legs.

Photo by Theresa Russell

Slide the shelf in between the legs at one end until the notches line up with all four legs. If the notches are not quite big enough to allow the shelf to fit flat on the frame, you may have to trim a little more from the shelf where it is making contact.

Photo by Theresa Russell

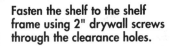

Fasten the shelf to the shelf frame using 2" drywall screws through the clearance holes.

Photo by Theresa Russell

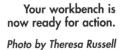

Your workbench is now ready for action.

Photo by Theresa Russell

Stock It

Organizing your tools, equipment, and supplies will be the next big step. First, place your workbench and any large power tools. Leave enough space to easily move around as you use the bench and the tools.

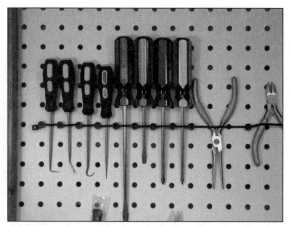

These tools are always visible and easy to reach.

Photo by Bungipeg

This is an easy way to organize and store your tools.

Photo by Gladiator

The wall space above the workbench is an ideal place to organize your hand tools on pegboard or nails and hooks. A rolling tool chest is another efficient way to organize tools. Shelves are ideal for frequently used tools and supplies; cabinets are good for storing power hand tools and containers that are infrequently used. Your needs, your budget, and the amount of space you have will determine your method of organization. Pegboards are relatively inexpensive, whereas rolling tool chests can be very expensive. Shelving and cabinets fall in between.

What exactly do you hang on the pegboard, put in the toolbox, or fill the cabinets with? You can find home maintenance tool sets of varying sizes and quality that contain a variety of tools to handle many repairs and projects.

Another option is to start with a few basic tools and add to them as you tackle more and more projects.

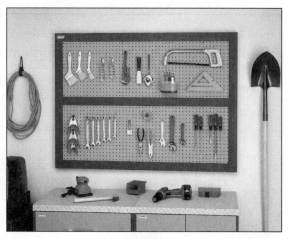

This homeowner has a hobby that requires a variety of pliers.

Photo by Coleman

Sometimes the repairs you need to do will help increase your collection of tools. Your vacuum cleaner needs some work and will require needle-nose pliers to repair it. You now have another tool in your collection.

The next few sections contain suggestions for starting your collections.

Tools

All homeowners should have most of these basic hand tools at their disposal:

- Hammer
- Assorted screwdrivers
- Combination wrenches
- Adjustable wrenches
- Assorted pliers
- Utility knife

- Tape measure
- Torpedo level
- Socket set
- Hex key wrench set
- C clamps and bar clamps
- Adjustable square
- Handsaw
- Hacksaw
- Sheet metal snips

You must have tools to determine how big something is, if it's level, and whether it's perpendicular and square.

Photo by Theresa Russell

Saws, snips, and knives are handy for cutting a variety of materials.

Photo by Theresa Russell

You can handle most any screw, bolt, or nut with these.

Photo by Alligator Board

Some more useful hand tools.

Photo by Theresa Russell

$ Loose Change _____

If you use a tool often and depend on it to reflect your craftsmanship, always purchase the highest quality available. On the other hand, if you use a tool infrequently and only for repairs and utility work, you may find adequate tools at discount tool stores.

Power tools are convenient to have. A drill is an essential tool in the home maintenance toolbox. Do consider the cordless varieties now available. Generally, the higher the voltage, the better. The basic power tools to have are as follows:

◆ Drill with a sufficient collection of bits

◆ Circular saw with a few different blades

◆ Jigsaw with a variety of blades

◆ Power sander with different grades of sandpaper

These handheld power tools make many tasks much easier.

Photo by Smithy

Hardware

Keeping some of the following items in the workshop might save you some trips to the store:

- Nails of various lengths and types
- Screws of various lengths and types
- Spare kitchen and bath cabinet hardware
- Spare window hardware
- Spare plumbing parts, such as washers, cartridges, wax rings for toilets, replacement fittings for garden hose
- Spare electrical parts, such as receptacles, switches, wire nuts, replacement plugs

You also can find prepackaged assortments of screws and nails to stock your workshop. As you do more and more projects, you will increase your collection of hardware with the extras from the job.

Loose Change

Using a plastic storage box about the size of a shoebox as your container, start a collection of odds and ends fasteners and hardware. Toss in the last couple of nails left in the big cardboard box, the extra mounting hardware that came with the mini-blinds, or the extra fasteners lying around. Many times, you can save yourself a trip to the hardware store by looking in the box.

Supplies

In our old houses, something is always being painted, remodeled, or updated. We are constantly using the following:

- Assorted grades of sandpaper
- Masking tape
- Duct tape

- Packing tape
- Cleaners and solvents
- Drop cloths
- Stir sticks
- Variety of paintbrushes
- Zip ties
- Bundling twine

First-Aid Kit

An essential and probably the first item you should stock your workspace with is a good, complete first-aid kit. If you have a kit elsewhere in the house, a second one is not a bad idea. At the very least, you should have band-aids, triple antibiotic ointment, and tweezers for splinters.

Keep the phone number and address of your local ER or urgent care center with your first-aid kit and keep current on your tetanus shots, too.

freedomRail.

Here is one way to conveniently organize small items.

Photo by Schulte

Safety Equipment

The well-equipped workspace starts with personal safety equipment. Following is a list of essential items that should be in any workplace:

◆ Eye protection

◆ Ear protection

◆ Masks for breathing protection

◆ Gloves

◆ Work apron

◆ Specific protection for certain types of work, such as welding or electrical work

◆ Protection from paint splatter, such as disposable coveralls and painter's caps

Keep at least three sets of eye protection available, so that one is always handy if you misplace another or if a friend comes over to help on a project. Have both nuisance dust masks and vapor masks ready to use when needed.

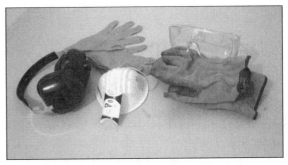

No home or workshop should be without these.

Photo by Theresa Russell

Keep guards or protective covers on all sharp tools. They protect you and prevent damage to the tool.

Finally, install a smoke detector at an appropriate location that won't contribute to false alarms from your workbench activities. Read the manufacturer's suggestions for mounting smoke detectors in garages and work areas. Finally, have a fully charged fire extinguisher mounted on a wall in an easy to grab place. It should be of the ABC type to handle any kind of fire.

Drive It Home

At my last physical, my doctor and I were discussing my woodworking activities. He mentioned that hearing becomes more easily damaged as we get older, and that I should be wearing hearing protection when using circular or miter saws. The intensity of noise produced by certain activities can cumulatively damage your hearing (often permanently).

Ear protection is available in both disposable plugs and earmuff styles. Keep a good supply of the disposable kind and use them when necessary. Protect your hands with work gloves. Use latex or nitrile gloves (avoid these if you are allergic to latex or nitrile) when working with solvents and leather work gloves for rough work. Use a floor pad designed to relieve stress on your feet and back while standing at your workbench, and make sure it is slip-resistant.

The Least You Need to Know

◆ Designate an area in your garage as a work area.

◆ Make your own work area if you don't have a dedicated space to work in.

◆ Upgrade your electric if it isn't adequate or safe.

◆ Work at a comfortable height on a solid workbench, rather than on the floor or on some makeshift surface.

◆ Keep your work area clean and stocked with the basic tools and supplies you need for home maintenance and repairs.

◆ Always use safety equipment to protect you and your home.

In This Part

Part 4

Ambitious Spaces

You have emptied your garage and thoroughly cleaned it. You've installed all the necessary storage units and accessories for your basic needs. You can easily park your car inside. Now you are ready to take the process a step further. Do you want to run a business out of your garage? Do you need a place to do some serious restoration of a car or boat? Do you need space for a hobby that's growing and taking over the house? Has your band become successful and now needs a regular practice space?

We show you some options for enhancing any space from carports to a three-car garage. In case you decide to do some of the work yourself, we include information about making structural and mechanical upgrades.

Finally, after all that work you've done, you will want to keep your new space looking like a new space. This section offers suggestions for maintaining your space and adjusting components to keep it working efficiently for you.

In This Chapter

- ◆ Making the best of your space
- ◆ Optimizing storage space
- ◆ Using your garage for something other than the car

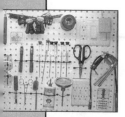  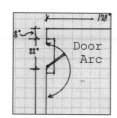   

Chapter 13

The One-Car Garage

The one-car garage, like most garages, does not have standard measurements. Some of them can barely fit a car into the space, requiring the driver to evict his passengers before driving the car into the garage. Don't despair if you have one of these small models. You can still do a few things to optimize the little space available. Let's take a look at the possibilities.

Best Use of the One-Car Garage

Remember, the primary purpose of the garage is for parking the car.

As pointed out before, there are good reasons to keep your car in the garage. It protects it from the elements. This alone can keep it at a moderate temperature and keep snow, rain, bird droppings, and other dirt off of it and keep it out of the way of stray toys, balls, or vehicles.

Some insurance companies may offer a lower rate for a car that is parked in a garage or driveway rather than on the street. Check with your agent to see what you could save. Before you decide to use your garage for something other than the car, consider how much extra in insurance premiums you will pay. Having the car in the garage also reduces the chance of theft, especially when additional theft-prevention elements are used.

A typical one-car garage.

Photo by Clopay

According to a study by the National Association of Realtors (NAR), the garage, along with laundry room, extra baths, and living room, are all important components of a desirable house.

Drive It Home _____

The value of your garage is 6 to 12 percent of your home, according to a National Association of Realtors study.

The garage itself can add extra value to a property, especially if it is in good condition. A garage that has been outfitted with extra storage options can move a house for sale to the top of the list if a buyer is considering similar houses at similar price points.

A garage designed with storage in mind is attractive to buyers.

Photo by Schulte

One thing to consider is the return on your investment in your garage. Don't expect to get back every dime that you put into it if you should sell your house. But also keep in mind that there is some personal value in having a place that lessens your stress level and works the way that you want it to. If you are considering selling, be sure that your garage is an attractive place.

Squeezing Out Space

You might be surprised at the space you can find if you just change where you park the car. Think about this. If you have a 12'×20' garage and a car such as the Nissan Pathfinder that measures 15.5 feet in length, you have an extra 4.5 feet in length. If you usually park all the way in the garage to within a foot of the back wall, you are leaving 3.5 feet on the garage door side of the garage, taking away useful space. If you park so that you leave a foot of clearance at the garage door side of the garage, you have 3.5 feet of storage space along the back wall.

Storage on the back wall doesn't have to extend all the way to floor. You could install cabinets or shelving high enough for the hood of your car to fit underneath. Just make sure whatever you install is sturdy. You don't want all the stuff to end up falling on your car.

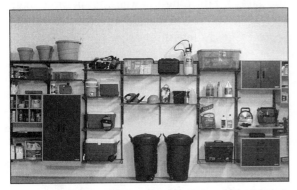

Putting things higher up leaves parking space for the car.

Photo by Schulte

Think about using the side walls for storage, too; although, depending on the size of your garage, you may have to let your passengers out before driving into the garage. You probably should consult with your primary passenger(s) to see whether they are okay with this before making the decision. You also probably will be able to access this space only when the car is parked elsewhere.

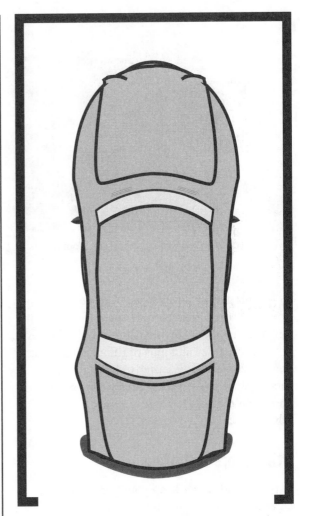

A car parked in the garage takes up this much space.

Photo by Robert Russell

Drive It Home

To be sure that you park the car in the same place, you can buy parking guides that either hang from the ceiling or attach to the wall. If your car fits tightly into your garage, you can buy bump guards that you put on the wall so that you won't damage the car door when it hits the wall.

Guards on the walls protect your doors.

Photo by Diamondlife

Is your garage unfinished? You are in luck. You have some great storage spaces available in between the studs. By installing simple shelves, you can organize all kinds of things until your heart is content. It is easier to hang things, too, because the studs are pretty obvious. Read about building shelves and hanging items in Chapter 10.

Other Storage Options

If you would rather keep your garage space clear for the car, you might want to consider getting a shed to store your things. This way you have easy access to your stuff and your car.

Another option to consider is putting the car under an easy-to-assemble garagelike shelter. Your car is protected from the elements and your garage can hold your stuff.

Examine your priorities. Although the garage was originally built for cars, Hewlett and Packard started a business in a one-car garage. Our guess is that the car got parked somewhere else.

Improvements

You may have just a few things that you want to store in your garage, but your main focus is getting the garage to look good. Several options will vastly improve the appearance of the garage. Finishing the walls, floor, or ceiling; adding light; moving or adding doors; or adding space are just a few things that you can do.

Finish the Walls and Floors

If the walls in your detached garage are unfinished, you might want to consider finishing them with some type of sheathing, usually drywall. You might be thinking that you can just put some paneling over the unfinished wall because that doesn't require so much work. Well, think twice about doing that. It will look good for a little while, but because there is little support behind the paneling, the panels will start to bow and look wavy. If you really want to install paneling, first hang drywall as a solid backing surface for the paneling. You don't have to finish the seams on the drywall. Then follow the instructions specific to the type of paneling you are installing.

T-111

One option is to use an exterior finish sheet good, such as *T-111*. No reason you can't use it inside. It comes in a variety of styles. It is rigid enough to be self-supporting when installed on studs that are 16 inches on center. The thicker versions should be installed on studs that are 24 inches on center. After this has been installed, you just finish it by priming and painting or leave it bare.

Definitions

T-111 is a board-and-batten style of finished sheet good and may be of plywood or composite construction. It comes in a variety of thicknesses, groove spacing, and textures.

You do not have to cover all four walls of your garage with this. If you just need one area that looks more finished or has a long expansive surface, this is certainly an option, too.

If your garage is attached and unfinished, you most likely need to install a fire barrier on any wall shared by the rest of the house and on the ceiling before installing any combustible wall covering. $^{5}/_{8}$-inch Type X drywall is the typical material used as a fire barrier. Check with your local building department to make sure your choice of material and your installation techniques are in compliance with the local building code.

Here are some basic tips for installing T-111:

◆ The sheets have lap joints on the long edges; so when two sheets are installed, the joint resembles one of the grooves. Make sure you bring the correct sides together for each joint.

◆ If you are covering an area that is taller than 8 feet, butt the short edges together. Then use a piece of z mold used in exterior application or a thin trim strip to cover the joint.

◆ When you cut the sheets using a circular saw, cut from the back side using a carbide-tipped blade, especially if you are cutting composite sheets.

◆ Use the fastener recommended by the manufacturer.

◆ Because you are installing inside, you don't have to use galvanized or stainless-steel fasteners. A larger finishing nail works nicely. They are typically driven in the grooves and set with a nail set to hide them. The grooves are commonly spaced 8 inches apart to accommodate both 16" and 24" stud spacing.

◆ You will find the whole installation experience faster and more pleasant if you use a pneumatic or power nail gun with the appropriate size fasteners.

◆ If you have trim around windows and doors, you may want to remove it and reapply it over the T-111, or measure carefully and butt up against it.

◆ If you have electrical fixtures, receptacles, or switches, remove the cover plates and fixtures and carefully measure and cut corresponding holes for each. If the electrical boxes have been mounted so that they protrude past the edge of the stud into the room by about a half inch or so, you are in luck and can carefully install the T-111 around the box. If the boxes have been mounted flush, you can get box extenders that will bring the box approximately flush with the new T-111 surface.

I would like to give you more detailed instructions about your project, but it is hard to when I can't see it from here.

Drywall

Another option is to hang drywall. If you do this, you might want to finish the ceiling, too. With T-111, you don't necessarily need to finish the ceiling.

Check with your local building department, regardless of whether your garage is attached or not, to make sure you will comply with the local building code.

Repairing Scratches and Dents

If your garage is already finished, it may need only a fresh coat of paint. If there is any damage to the drywall, which is likely because the garage tends to take a little more abuse than the rest of your house, you can just repair it. Depending on the extent of the dents, cracks, and holes, you may only need a small amount of drywall compound and a wide putty knife. Spread the compound over the damage, trying to keep it slightly below the plane of the wall or even with the wall. It may take a couple of coats to build it up. Lightly sand the repair to feather the edges and bring the new compound flush with the wall.

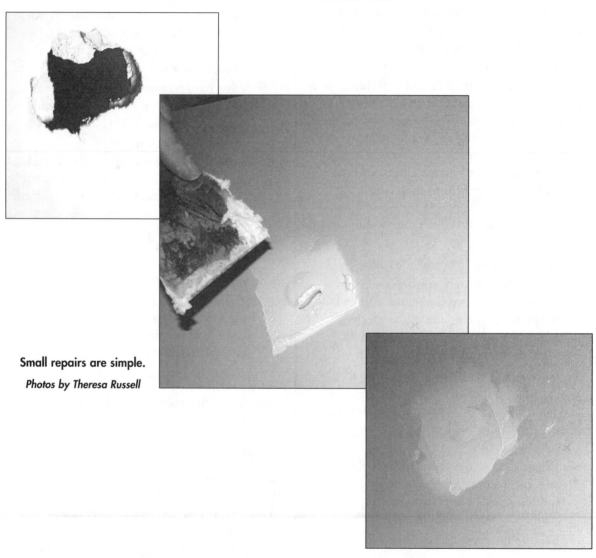

Small repairs are simple.

Photos by Theresa Russell

If you have a larger crack or a hole, you may be able to reinforce the compound with joint tape. For a large hole you may need to fill in with a new piece of drywall cut to fit the opening. The large home improvement centers sell all the materials you need, including some repair kits with interesting fasteners and techniques for filling in larger holes.

Floors

Painting a floor can give it new life. If you are using regular garage floor paint, be sure to follow the instructions on the can for preparing the surface.

A coat of floor paint improves the look of this garage.

Photo by Erik Russell

A fresh coat of paint results in a noticeable difference and cleans up the room. If you are thinking of using epoxy and doing it yourself, you might want to think twice. Some experts think that the consumer-grade epoxy is not as durable as the professional grade. They claim that *hot tire pick-up* is a problem and that the epoxy will chip and peel. They recommend having experts do this. Ask around at your local paint store for opinions on this product.

Definitions

When tires become warm and even hot from friction caused by contact with the road, you get **hot tire pick-up**. Tires can become hot enough, especially in the summer, to soften the paint on your garage floor so much that it actually peels off.

Another flooring option is a rollout covering that is quick and easy to install and clean. You can cover the entire floor or just sections of it as you see necessary.

It is a practical and durable covering made of a high-strength polymer. If you are considering pouring a new floor or repairing a significantly damaged old one, go to Chapter 17.

Tile is yet another option for your garage floor.

Rolled-out flooring is a quick and easy option for improving the surface of your garage floor.

Photo by BLT

See how dramatic a simple change can be.

Photos by BLT

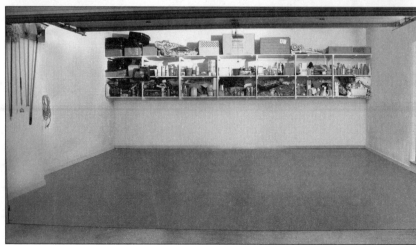

Tile is durable as a flooring material.

Photo by Gladiator

Let There Be Light

Often the only light in the garage comes from a window or from a single bulb in the middle of the ceiling. When you are hunting for something in one of your storage units or on a shelf, it helps to have enough light to see what you are doing. A ceiling light in the center of the garage just doesn't do it. If you have outlets in your garage, you can use clip-on lamps and keep them in strategic places around the garage. If you don't have any outlets in the garage, you need to consider other options. Often it is the detached garage that lacks electricity. Read about how to upgrade/install electrical in Chapter 16.

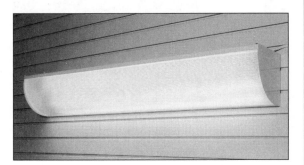

Good lighting puts less strain on the eyes.

Photo by GarageTek

Remember that good lighting contributes to safety. An exterior light at exit doors is a good idea. Consider adding motion detectors to these so that they come on and off automatically.

Drive It Home

The incandescent light bulb is inefficient. Replacing this style of light bulb with fluorescent bulbs will save energy. They even come in a screw-in style to easily fit into your current fixtures. Using one third of the wattage that you would for your usual light bulbs, they last much longer.

Cutting out a spot in the wall to insert a window usually involves some serious structural modification. If you want to add windows, go to Chapter 17. If you don't want to do such a big project, changing out a solid entry door and replacing it with another that has windows will add light.

The same holds true for the main garage door. Adding a door with windows will obviously help with the lighting situation. These simple changes are especially helpful in an unwired garage.

This garage door has windows that allow light into the space.

Photo by Clopay

The Doors

A coat of paint on both the service doors and the large garage door where the car enters can spruce up the look of your garage in a jiffy. Because the garage door is a prominent space and easily noticeable, especially when it belongs to an attached garage, the door can have a significant impact on the look of your house. Choose your colors wisely for this important element. If your door is just worn out, you need to replace it. Read in Chapter 17 about this.

If you live in a hurricane-prone area, you may want to consider reinforcing the door so that it offers some wind resistance. You can find kits that have everything you need to do this.

Add Space

As discussed previously, you don't need to physically add on to the garage to add usable space. It is critical to look at every nook and cranny for extra space if your garage is small.

Screen It

No screened-in porch? There may be one right in your yard. During the warmer months, the thought of sitting on a screened porch or having a spot for the kids to play ranks high on many lists. If you can keep your car out of the garage during the warm weather, you can reassign its primary purpose to becoming an enclosed patio room.

The addition of a screen door makes an instant patio room.

Photo by Frank Pace

Several manufacturers make screens specifically designed for garages. They are simple enough to install and keep the bugs out, the air flowing, and totally change the ambience of your garage.

After you have your screen on, organize your inside space like an outside patio. This space could equally be your summer office or a rec room for the kids to play in. Use your imagination.

Attic Space

Look up to see what kind of space is available. Some one-car garages have low-pitched roofs. Obviously, flat-roofed garages have no attic space. A low-pitched roof may allow enough space for smaller and flatter objects such as snowboards, skis, or paddles. Installing a floorboard will make more usable space, but be sure that boards will fit between the joists with enough clearance to lay flat. We talk more about attic storage in Chapter 10.

Don't forget the ceiling. As discussed in Chapter 10, there are a lot of things that can be hung. Even if you have a flat roof, if you have a car rather than an SUV, you may be able hang things such as your family's bicycles from the ceiling.

A new product is the snap-together tile from Attic Dek. What is nice about this is that individual tiles are small enough to get up into the attic. You can put this on just a small area of the floor.

If you are getting up by ladder, be sure that you leave enough space for you to get in that space. If your area has a low ceiling, just tile what you can reach. Be careful when putting things beyond the area that you have floored.

Bonus Extra Half

Any size garage with an extra half is a real bonus. You can use that space just like any other room. The possibilities are endless. The only limitations are most of the things that we have previously discussed. You can use this space as an office, a laundry room, an exercise room, or for just about anything that you want it for as long as you have a safe space that includes whatever utilities or enhancements you need for the space.

Continue to Chapter 15 to read about more possibilities for the extra half of your garage.

The Least You Need to Know

◆ Moving your regular parking space may increase the storage potential of your garage.

◆ Be open to the possibility of parking your car elsewhere to open up options for your garage.

◆ Replace your garage door with a screen for outdoor living during the summer.

◆ Improve lighting with windows in doors.

◆ Install flooring for attic storage.

◆ Finish the walls with T-111 as an alternative to hanging drywall.

◆ Repair drywall damage before painting.

In This Chapter

- ◆ Deciding how to use the space
- ◆ How to use the space if you don't park the car there
- ◆ Creating a new functional space

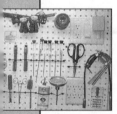  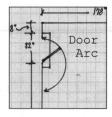   

Chapter 14

The Two-Car Garage

The two-car garage, like any other garage, has no standard dimensions. The main prerequisite for a two-car garage is obvious—it can hold two cars. Sometimes the way the garage holds the two cars can be problematic. A smaller-size garage might have just enough space for two cars to park, but nothing else. It could be so tight that great care needs to be taken when opening car doors. At the other extreme is the spacious two-car garage. Plenty of room awaits for storing anything you want. The storage space on the walls, ceiling, and attic is similar to what is in the one-car garage. The same concepts apply. The two-car garage has a longer back wall that offers even more storage space. The attic and ceiling space are larger, too. Review the last chapter for tips on storage.

Because of the increased size, you have more possibilities for doing modifications in the layout or adding proprietary spaces. This is often done while sacrificing some parking space. If your garage will be used solely for parking cars, you need read no further. If you will use your garage for parking, but have an oversized garage, go to Chapter 15 and read about the extra half.

Be Careful

You know the importance of storing your cars in a sheltered spot like the garage. Sometimes priorities in life change. Your garage has so much space and is cheaper to modify than other rooms in your house. You need to decide once again what your priorities are.

Photo by Overhead

If you don't have rules that require you to keep your cars inside your garage, you have some options for transforming your garage into a more functional space. It isn't necessarily a black-and-white decision. One car could be parked in the garage and the other on the street. The garage could be just a winter parking space that adapts to a different use in the summer. It could act as a multifunctional room with separate areas for parking and for another designated purpose such as a summer playroom for the kids or a place to build a new business empire.

Modifications

Changing your garage space to provide a more efficient area for your needs can be something very simple such as using a certain area as an office or play area. It can be more complicated such as building a partition wall, which is discussed later. It can also be very complicated such as totally converting the space into a different room, which is beyond the scope of this book.

Simple modifications include using an area of the garage as a dedicated space. You could have achieved this by using a corner of your garage, for instance, as a home office or workout room. But what if there is an obstruction or something else that prevents contiguous space? You could have also used linear space like a long narrow space along the wall, which is perfect for a small area, but could also be too spread out for certain projects.

Drive It Home

You can construct a quick and easy "wall" from door slabs connected with removable pin hinges. Use hollow-core door slabs purchased at a discount building supply store. Screw a couple of hinges between every two doors and zigzag them across the floor. You can make the wall as long as you need, and you can shorten or lengthen it by removing or adding pins to the hinges.

With the space available from removing one car from the garage, it is possible to have your own "room" for whatever you would like it to be. The walls can be real or an illusion created by the use of vertical elements such as screens, tall cabinets, or even hanging fabric. Adding things such as wall hangings (that doesn't mean the shovel or rake that you hung on the wall) or putting down a carpet to identify an area will give the space some boundaries.

$ **Loose Change**

Carpeting in a garage usually does not last as long as carpeting inside your home. You may decide not to do a complete installation with a quality pad. In this case, consider using remnants from a discount carpet store.

If you have the time, you can almost finish the entire half of the garage. Don't forget that if you are finishing an unfinished garage, there are certain guidelines to follow for safety and fire-code reasons. See Chapters 16 and 17 for an in-depth discussion of this.

If your walls are already finished, you can improve the appearance of the area by painting them. Follow the steps in Chapter 9 to prep and paint your walls properly.

Arranging your furniture, equipment, or supplies in a way that encloses the space will have just that effect. For instance, if you repair bicycles on the side, you could have a workbench on one wall, a bike stand on another wall or against the imaginary wall in the center of the garage, and a pegboard with tools on the back wall.

An artist would have supplies on the two solid walls and an easel on the illusionary wall that is in the middle of the garage. A light that is centered in the area also helps delineate the space and provides illumination to make the area a safe place to work.

It is certainly possible to totally transform your garage into another space. One fellow built a brewery in his two-car garage. Be careful about doing this. Should you be thinking of selling your home in the future and this is your only garage, you may be diminishing the salability of your home.

This separate area is useful for a bike mechanic.

Photo by Gladiator

Now here's a different use for the garage. Notice that the kids do still get to play Ping-Pong here.

Photos by John Marioni

Our son bought a property that had commercial zoning. The house is residential, but his two-car detached garage was rented out and will be used in the future as a studio for a personal trainer. Depending on where you live, this could be a possibility. There are no neighborhood associations where he lives, so he parks his cars in the driveway or on the street. The money he makes on the rental goes toward his mortgage.

Other people have similar arrangements. If you have a two-car detached garage or any size garage that you don't park a car in, you could rent it out to somebody for storage or as a parking spot. Check with your local zoning board, insurance company, and lawyer to see what types of responsibilities and liabilities this entails. It may not turn out to be something you want to do in the long run.

Partition Walls

A real wall has the advantage of obviously blocking off the parking area of the garage and converting the enclosed space to resemble any other room in the house, if it is done correctly. The first thing to do before installing a center wall is to check out local building codes. Especially if your garage is detached, you need to evaluate its structural integrity. The addition of a center wall in this case could actually add support and make it more structurally stable.

Here is a plan for building a partition wall:

1. Identify any fixtures, switches, receptacles, or structural components that might be in the way.

2. Take careful, accurate measurements of the space in which you intend to install the wall. Take multiple measurements of the height, because your garage floor may have a slope and the ceiling may be level.

3. This will be a long wall, so it will probably be easier to construct in two sections. Decide on a convenient length for each section.

4. Typical construction using 2×4s would consist of a bottom plate, a top plate, and studs in between placed 16 inches apart. Lay the top and bottom plate next to each other flat on the garage floor. Start at one end and mark off a stud placement every 16 inches. The end stud will cover the first $1\frac{1}{2}$ inches, and each stud after that will be centered on the 16" marks extending $\frac{3}{4}$ inch before and after the mark. Use a square and draw a line across both plates at each of those before and after marks.

5. Move the plates apart and rotate them on edge with the marks facing each other. Place a stud that has been cut to the ceiling height minus $3\frac{1}{4}$ inches between each of the marks. Nail through the plates into the studs using two 16d common nails at each end of the stud. Drive the nails approximately $\frac{3}{4}$ inch from the edge.

6. Stand the wall up. It should be a snug fit. Move it into position. Use a level and get it vertical. Secure the bottom plate into the concrete floor using some type of concrete anchor or concrete screw that was discussed in the installation challenges of Chapter 10. Locate the ceiling joists and secure the top plate into them using $3\frac{1}{2}$" or 4" drywall screws.

7. Repeat the process for the next wall section.

It's sometimes easier to build the wall outside.

Photo by Theresa Russell

A finished wall with a header for French doors.

Photo by Theresa Russell

After that wall is built, you may want to insulate it or install soundproofing material before closing it up. You may want to add additional electrical outlets. You can hang drywall or cover the wall with other materials including pegboard, slat wall, or T-111.

Utility/Laundry Space

You could squeeze a washer and dryer in the garage if you have some space. Think about using the space on the back wall, if it is convenient to plumbing sources. Obviously, if you will be using only half of your garage for parking, you have a large area to install a laundry. For this purpose, using the half of the garage adjacent to the house is ideal because it most likely abuts a kitchen, which already has plumbing.

We lived in a house that had a detached garage that wasn't too far behind the house. It had a side room that was set up for plumbing. So it isn't impossible to add laundry facilities to a detached garage. The big issues in this case are having electrical hookups, gas line if you have a gas dryer, and water for the washer. Adding any of these utilities will cost some money.

Specialty Workshop

That extra side of the garage makes a perfect spot for a woodworking shop. All tools and equipment can be stored in one spot. Because of the extra space, it isn't necessary to move larger tools, such as band saws and table saws, to a different place each night because there are no worries about a place for parking the car.

The garage is a possible spot for the laundry.

Photo by Schulte

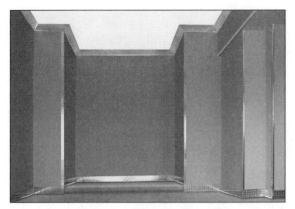

Who says that a garage can't look elegant?

Photo by Diamondlife

Such a workshop can be outfitted to look just like any other room in the house. Crown molding and baseboard trim give the room a finished look. Flooring can be added on this half of the garage for aesthetics or for comfort.

Studio/Home Office

If you work out of your home, you have a bedroom office or another small space that you call your office. If you are lucky, you have an entire room set up as an office. That is not always the case. A home office can easily operate out of the garage. Be sure that you have outlets for your computer and office equipment. A temperature-regulating system, whether it is central, window air, or a space heater, will add to your comfort level and keep your equipment in good working order.

Studios often house messy activities. Painting, pottery, and stained-glass cutting all leave a mess behind. This type of area will do well with a concrete floor. You don't need to worry about ruining the finish on the floor or splattering paint on the walls. Only you can decide how "clean" your space needs to be.

If you do use a part of the garage as an office, check with your tax advisor about tax advantages. Keep in mind that deducting parts of your house for business now will have an effect on taxes when you sell your house.

Continue to Chapters 16 and 17 if you are planning on doing major structural or mechanical enhancements to this space.

The Least You Need to Know

- Consider the advantages of not parking the car in the garage.
- Modify half of the garage to meet your needs.
- Define and create a new space.
- Avoid making extra space extra messy.

In This Chapter

◆ Increasing the utility of a carport

◆ Freeing up space in your house

◆ Exploring new uses for the extra half

◆ Optimizing your storage

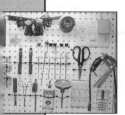

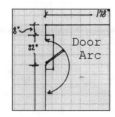

Chapter 15

Special Spaces

Some houses have special spaces of their own. The carport is one such space. It is a minimal garage. At the other extreme is the garage with the extra half added to it. This configuration offers lots of extra space and new possibilities for assigning alternative uses to that space or parts of it.

The Carport

Some houses don't have garages, but instead have carports. In many cases the carport is attached to the house, just as the porte cochère of old. In fact, the carport is a modern version of the porte cochère. A carport can also be a freestanding, detached unit.

As discussed in Chapter 1, the carport can range from an awning or roof held up by four posts to a more substantial structure that looks more like a garage with two or three of its walls missing. Some carports do have a structure for storage, somewhat like a shed at one end.

A basic-style carport.

Photo by Theresa Russell

A carport with a back storage room.

Photo by Theresa Russell

Enclosures

If you want to make your carport a patio house, you can do this simply by adding screens. You can do this using a frame or a simple roll-down screen. This provides a nice place to relax outside or to have a summer "porch" for dining. The options are limited only by your imagination.

You could consider making the carport structurally sound and enclosing it to become a full-fledged garage. This is a major project that is beyond the scope of the book. Contact a contractor and get estimates if you are thinking of doing this.

Secure Storage

The big concern about using your carport for storage is safety. We live in a neighborhood where we can leave our garden tools outside and nobody will bother them. However, that is not the case everywhere. It is something that you need to consider before you decide to use the carport as a summer workshop or a place to store expensive tools.

The obvious solution is to not put anything there that you can't afford to lose. Another solution is to buy containers that can be locked. You also can put something around your tools to lock them in place.

The Bonus Half

If you are the lucky owner of a garage with an extra half, you have plenty of options for utilizing that space. This can be an extension of your house and a place that could be used to free up space in your home. You could convert that space into a utility room and put your laundry there or move your furnace and water heater. This space is ideal for a home office, workshop, or maybe even a second kitchen or playroom for the kids.

Free Up Interior Home Space

Whether your plus-size garage is attached or detached, the space lends itself to an extra storage space that could free up some space inside your house.

The extra half adds plenty more space.

Photo by Theresa Russell

Let your imagination run wild with this extra space.

Photo by Wesson Garages

If your kids play sports, it could be used as a place to store their equipment. A climate-controlled space could work as a practice room for an individual or a band.

Laundry

As mentioned in an earlier chapter, if the extra half of your garage is close to the plumbing system in the house, putting a laundry in this area is a possibility. If your current laundry is nonexistent or is in the basement of your house, you can install it in this space, which would be more convenient. Even though there will be some cost involved, think about what you will save in time and money, especially if you are currently going to the Laundromat.

Utilities

This extra half space could be the place to put utilities, especially if you were planning on upgrading your residential system anyway. If you don't have gas, water, or electric nearby, these could be a costly option. However, if your hot water heater is taking up precious space in your house, you could move it here. This is also where you can install utilities specifically for the garage. Usually a garage needs its own circulation system that is independent of the house.

Workshop, Home Office, and More

Use this space as you would the space of a two-car garage divided in half. You are lucky because your garage might already have a wall dividing the extra space from the rest of the garage. If not, and you would like to have a partition wall, go back to Chapter 14 and read about installing a dividing wall.

The options for using this space are limited only by your imagination. Whether you dream of having a dedicated workshop, a home office, a pool house, or a play area for the kids, you can use this spot to give your home the feel of a much larger house.

Think about your dream spot and take action to make it happen.

The Least You Need to Know

◆ Modify your carport into a more useful space.

◆ Optimize space in your home by moving some utilities into the garage.

◆ Treat that extra half as you would when repurposing half of a two-car garage.

◆ Maximize your storage options in that extra half.

In This Chapter

- The basics of your mechanical systems
- Upgrading your mechanical systems
- Safety issues
- Budget considerations

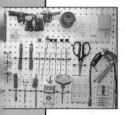  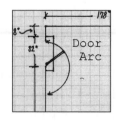   

16

Upgrading Mechanical Systems

You've decided to go all out and create the ultimate garage. You want to upgrade the electric in the garage, run water to the garage, and provide heat in the winter and cooling in the summer. You've already checked with your local building inspector (as well as other organizations you are responsible to) to find out what is allowed. So let's get to work on some upgrades.

Budget Considerations

The previous chapters in the book have helped you determine what you need, what will work for you, and whether you can and will install the solution. After you finalized your design, you may have found that some significant electrical, plumbing, or HVAC modifications are needed for your garage makeover.

Before you start on any of these projects, get three estimates for each job. You may find a general contractor who can handle the entire project or you may go with individual tradespeople. As you estimate labor and materials costs for your garage solution, it will be informative and worthwhile to get a range of estimates for all the variations you may be considering. If you are thinking of bringing electric to a detached building, you could be in for a surprise. Sometimes it is possible to run electric service underground to the garage from a house service line. Moving utility poles or adding new service can be quite costly.

Drive It Home _____

Contractors can easily estimate time and labor costs for specific jobs from the experience of having done these jobs before. You can estimate the cost of your project by using one of the estimate books containing estimated labor and construction costs for specific remodeling jobs. You should be able to find these at any larger bookstore or any home improvement center.

The garage is an option for the laundry.

Photo by Theresa Russell

If you want to have running water in the garage, try to place your new sink, laundry hookups, or other plumbing fixtures as close as possible to the existing plumbing in the rest of the house. The farther away from water lines and drains you want to have water, the more it will cost.

$ Loose Change _____

In the past few years, many home improvement centers have made arrangements with professional installers to provide installation of the products they sell. This can be a good place to start collecting the quotes for your modifications. Many of the products they sell have labor estimates right alongside the prices posted on the racks.

Carefully describe your project, using sketches or drawings that accurately indicate all necessary dimensions for the modifications you need. The larger the scope and scale of your project's modifications, the more advisable it is for you to have your plans reviewed by a professional. If you are going to do most or all of the work yourself, at the very least you should take your plans to your local building department. Any inspector can make sure you are in compliance with all the local building codes. You want to be sure that your plans meet the health and safety requirements of the local building code and that there are no issues that may significantly increase costs.

The materials costs could vary from less than a hundred dollars for adding an electrical circuit to several thousand for a complete climate-control system with air filtration. Carefully review the materials lists if you are working with a contractor or a professional tradesperson. Shop around for the best prices if you are doing the work yourself. Get accurate estimates from the professionals about the amount of time involved in completing your needed modification and the cost of the labor. Make sure your estimates are accurate.

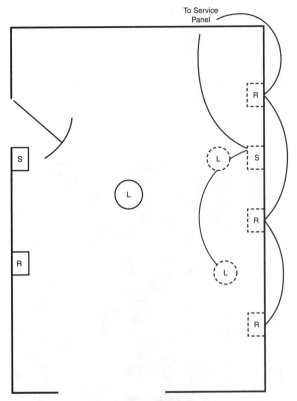

Sketch of electrical plans.

Sketch by Robert Russell

Drive It Home

The general rule of thumb is that labor costs comprise about 60 percent of the costs of a remodeling project. However, these costs can vary widely depending on whether you are using union labor, in what area of the country you live, whether rural or big city, or if you are in a booming construction market. Unless you live in Hawaii or Alaska, where transportation costs add significantly to products, you should find much less variability in the cost of materials.

If you want to consider doing the work yourself, you can use this estimate as a guide. The rule of thumb is that the do-it-yourselfer will take two to three times as long as a professional

to complete a task. The reason being that you will work slower and more carefully and, yes, you will need to read the instructions.

So to ensure that you will obtain accurate estimates, you need accurate descriptions of your modifications, a go ahead from your building inspector, and accurate labor and material estimates.

Electric and Lighting

Electricity can be a pretty scary subject, but it is something that you can't live without. You need it to power your lights, power your tools and appliances, and provide power for other functions in your home. Your garage may or may not have electrical service. If it does have service, it may or may not suffice for your garage solution. You may need to increase lighting or add some circuits. You may only need to replace some fixtures, switches, or receptacles. Whatever the scope of the work you need done, it helps to know some basics about the electrical service in your home and garage so that you can work safely if you decide to do some of the work yourself or so that you can better understand what the electrician is doing.

Electricity 101

To begin with, here are some electrical terms you should know:

- **Voltage.** The electrical force or pressure, measured in volts, that causes current to flow in a circuit
- **Amperage.** The movement of the electrical current in a circuit, measured in amps
- **Resistance.** The opposition to the flow of current in a circuit, measured in ohms
- **Wattage.** The power used by an electrical device, measured in watts and calculated by multiplying volts times amps

We can think of electricity as water flowing in a pipe. The voltage is the water pressure, the amperage is the size of the pipe, and the resistance is the restriction we could place at the end of the pipe. We can then think of the wattage as the work done by the water flow.

You should also know these additional terms:

◆ **Hot.** Anything such as wiring that carries voltage

◆ **Neutral.** Anything such as wiring that returns current to its source at zero voltage

◆ **Ground.** Anything such as wiring that conducts current to the earth in the event of a short circuit

◆ **Circuit.** An unbroken loop of electrical current flowing through wires, fixtures, and electrical devices

◆ **Circuit breaker.** A safety switch that interrupts the flow of current through a circuit in the event of a short or overload

◆ **Fuse.** A safety device that interrupts the flow of current through a circuit in the event of a short or overload

Let's start outside your house. Somewhere, not too far away, is a transformer that reduces voltage to 120 volts, feeding into your house through two hot wires and a neutral wire. These lines pass through a meter and terminate in the service panel located somewhere in your home. It is usually located in the basement, the garage, or a utility room.

The service panel is the beginning and end of each of the circuits in your home. There may be subpanels connected to the service panel that provide a beginning and end for a select set of circuits. This is common in detached garages. The electricity must complete a circuit flowing through the hot wire and back to the neutral. Most of the circuits in your home branch off one of the hot wires coming into your house.

Either a circuit breaker or a fuse protects each branch. This is designed to be the weakest part of the circuit, so that when something goes wrong, the circuit breaker trips or the fuse blows. When the cause of the problem is determined and fixed, the breaker can be reset or the fuse replaced.

A typical service panel.
Photo by Robert Russell

Some appliances or equipment, such as electric dryers, electric ranges, air-conditioning units, or large air compressors, may require 240 volts. This is achieved by using both hot wires in a circuit. A ground wire is typically included in a circuit to provide a safe path for any electricity that leaks out of the circuit. Ground wires are either bare or covered in green insulation, neutral wires are usually covered in white insulation, and hot wires are usually covered in black or red insulation.

Whereas most of the circuits carry 120 volts, the circuit breaker or fuse will determine the maximum amps. Lighting circuits are typically 15 amps, and receptacle circuits are either 15 or 20 amps. Lighting and receptacle circuits should be separate circuits. Perhaps you have used a power tool and watched the lights dim. The lights and receptacle were probably on the same circuit. You may be able to wire in a new circuit for either the lights or the receptacles by adding a new breaker to the service panel.

This brings us to an important part of our lesson. You need to determine the status of your service panel and whether new circuits can be added. Older homes have service limited to 100 amps, or even as low as 60 amps. Newer homes have 200-amp service or higher. The main shutoff breaker should be marked with the maximum amps or the panel should have a label indicating the maximum amps. Add up the numbers on the individual circuit breakers or fuses and see whether you have reached the maximum.

At this point, you may want to have an electrician advise you on your options. You might consider replacing the service panel with a larger one, you might be able to add a subpanel, or you might need to upgrade the service into your home. These possibilities are typically best left to experienced electricians. In all cases, you or your electrician must obtain the necessary permits and follow your local building code.

> **Drive It Home**
>
> The most common way to run electrical service to a detached garage is by digging a trench and burying electric cable specifically designed for this purpose. One end is connected to the main lines inside your home's service panel, and the other end terminates in a subpanel mounted on the inside of your garage. Local building codes precisely dictate how this can be done.

Wiring

Let's discuss wiring now. The most common electrical wiring you will find in recently built homes and for use in remodeling is Type *NM* 12-2 *G* or 14-2 *G*.

> **Definitions**
>
> **NM,** or nonmetallic, is usually a thin but very durable plastic.
>
> **G,** or gauge, is the size of the wire. The smaller the number, the larger the wire diameter and so the more current it will carry.

This common wire cable used for residential wiring contains two insulated wires and a bare ground wire, all sheathed in a plastic cover. The 12 gauge is typically used for receptacles, and the 14 gauge is used for lights. The cable terminates in the service panel and runs through walls, above ceilings, and under floors to reach fixtures, switches, and receptacles. Proper installation involves attaching the wires to studs and joists and avoiding potential problems from fasteners used to install drywall and other coverings. Your local building department will have specific instructions on how to install the cable.

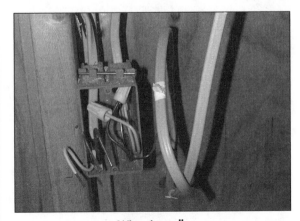

Wires in wall.

Photo by Robert Russell

Whenever the cable ends or a junction must be made, an electrical box should be used. A light fixture or a receptacle may be mounted in a terminal box. A switch is installed in a switch box, and a junction box is used to protect the connection of two or more cables.

All of this should be done according to the National Electrical Code (NEC). Local building codes will follow this and may apply additional requirements. Your local building department can provide you with the resources you need in order to understand and apply these codes. The codes have been written and are enforced to protect you and the future occupants of your house.

Let's Get Wired

Let's work through a typical situation you might find yourself in. You have an older garage with one receptacle in an inconvenient location. You find yourself climbing up a ladder to plug things into the socket that holds the light bulb in the middle of the ceiling. You could definitely use some additional electrical outlets. If that's the only light in your garage, some additional light fixtures wouldn't hurt.

Drive It Home

Most local building codes allow you to do some of the electrical work in your home. All work must be done in compliance with the National Electrical Code (NEC). Local codes may add additional requirements and restrictions.

You've checked with your local building department and found that you are allowed to do electrical work in your own home. You've found out which materials you must use and how to properly install them.

You want to identify the correct circuit in your service panel if it isn't marked. Have an assistant watch the ceiling light and a lamp plugged into the receptacle, while you carefully remove and replace fuses or flip circuit breakers one by one until either one or both lights go out. You now know which circuits these are on, and you can turn them off so you can safely work on extending the wiring for extra outlets and lights in the garage.

Warning Light

You may be tempted to "just be careful" and not bother turning off the electricity to the circuit in the service panel. Those are famous last words. Don't even consider doing it. Take the extra time to walk over to the service panel, and take the time to identify the circuit if it isn't marked.

Wiring "hot" is not worth the risk.

If you have a finished garage, you have a few options. You can either open up the wall or ceiling by cutting a path where you need to run the wire cable and patch it afterwards, or you can attempt to "fish" it through using an electrical *fish tape*.

Definitions

Electrical **fish tapes** are used to pull wires through closed walls and conduit. Careful planning can result in minimal holes cut into walls to fish wire through holes drilled in studs or wall plates.

Another possibility is to run the wire on the outside of the wall using special metal or plastic channel. Your local electrical code will specify exactly what you can and can't do.

If you do not plan on tearing into your walls, you can install old work boxes, also known as remodeler's boxes. You will first need to find the studs using a stud finder, and then, using the template that came with the box, cut a hole in the drywall using a keyhole saw. Pull the wires through the hole, insert them into the box, and then place the box inside the hole and against the stud. Mount the box to the stud.

If you have an unfinished garage, you can use new work boxes and mount them where you need them in accordance with the code requirements. Pull wire cable into the boxes to complete the circuit, making sure to secure the cable as required.

Install your fixtures, receptacles, and switches according to the directions that should be included with each. The directions are written to follow the NEC. If you are confused, feeling less confident, or intimidated by making a connection inside the service panel, hire an electrician.

If you plan to use a kiln for firing ceramics, have an electric dryer or range, or use some larger power tools in the garage, you need 240-volt service there. This is probably a job you will want to leave for an experienced electrician.

Warning Light

You shut off the power to the circuit you are going to be working on. Good. Don't ever assume that the circuit is dead without testing it. Use a plug-in tester or an inductive tester. Decent ones can be purchased at any home improvement center for under $20. Well worth the investment.

Also don't assume that the wiring in your home or garage has been done according to code or even close to some logical manner, especially in an older home that may have had several owners. I have found bare grounds that were hot and reversed hot and neutral wires. Please be careful.

Ground Fault Interruption

Because your garage can open to a wet or damp situation, it is considered a wet area and should have ground fault interruption (GFI) installed at every outlet. If you already have adequate outlets, this is a minor project that you could do or hire it done. It can help you rest a little easier knowing that these receptacles will cut power if there is any short in the circuit.

The GFI receptacle is a safety device.

Photo by Theresa Russell

The current flowing through the hot and neutral wires in a circuit should be the same. If there is a difference in the current, it could be that a person has come in contact with the hot wire or a malfunctioning electrical device and is being shocked. A normal circuit breaker or fuse may not detect this condition. A GFI receptacle or circuit breaker will trip when it detects 5 milliamps of current leakage in about $1/40$ of a second. These are amazing devices that disconnect both the hot and neutral lines of a circuit. Although a ground wire is recommended for installation, they can be installed as replacements for old two-prong outlets.

There are two basic ways to go about installing this protection. Perhaps the easiest is to install a special GFI circuit breaker in your service panel. This will protect every receptacle and fixture on the entire circuit. The other way is to install a GFI receptacle at every outlet location in the garage. This a little more expensive, but makes life a little easier when you need to find where the problem is. Only one receptacle will be shut down, unlike the entire circuit being shut down by the GFI breaker in the service panel. A variation of this is to install the GFI receptacle at the first outlet on the garage circuit and then connect the rest of the circuit to the *load terminals*. This is the least-expensive way to go and provides protection for all the other outlets.

![ABC Definitions]

Definitions

When you look at the back of your GFI receptacle, you will see terminals marked as load and line. The **load terminals** will carry electricity to the remaining receptacles on the circuit and the **line terminals** will bring electricity into this receptacle.

To do the actual installation of the receptacle, you must first turn off the power to the circuit, and then remove the old receptacle. Make sure there is room for the GFI receptacle, because they are significantly larger than ordinary receptacles. Connect the wires to the line terminals for the first receptacle in the circuit, and the other wires for the rest of the circuit to the load terminals if your old receptacle had them. Install the new receptacle in the box and test it before putting the new cover plate on.

If you are not comfortable with working with electricity, call an electrician for all of these projects.

Simple Electrical Solutions

If you just need extra outlets for your workbench, consider getting a heavy-duty power strip. This is an easy and inexpensive way to add electric convenience. Be sure that you don't overload the plugs, and that your current service is able to handle your power tools or whatever you plug in.

Getting Help

We've barely scratched the surface of what electrical modifications you may need in your garage. Some electrical components have more complicated jobs, such as three-way switches or ceiling fans with lights. We didn't discuss other types of wire cable and coverings such as armored cable and conduit. Other modifications, such as HVAC installation, have a major electrical component to them.

If you feel confident enough to tackle some or all of your electrical projects, you can usually find a wealth of knowledge and advice in the electrical sections of the home improvement stores. Often the people working in those departments will be retired electricians or electrical contractors, or at the very least, advanced do-it-yourselfers who are willing to help you succeed in your project. Go in with your drawings and an open mind, and you should find most of what you need. Just remember that your local building department does have the last word and should always be consulted.

Water and Plumbing

You are sick of going to the Laundromat every week and want to have a laundry center in that extra space in the garage. With the stackable washer and dryer pairs, you have a few more options (because you only need enough space for one appliance rather than two). Ideally, this area should be close to other plumbing systems in the house. This, of course, applies to an attached garage. If there is a bathroom or kitchen adjacent to the garage, running the plumbing will be a lot simpler than if there are no pipes or water lines nearby.

Plumbing 101

Before we start tearing into walls looking for pipes, let's go through some of the basics as we did for electricity. If you are experienced with plumbing modifications, go get your hammer and crowbar. Otherwise, we try to give you an understanding of how the plumbing in your home works and help you decide what to do, how much to do on your own, and when to call an experienced plumber.

The plumbing in your home is made up of two independent systems, the water distribution system and drain-waste-vent system (DWV). The water distribution system is further divided into two separate systems: hot water and cold water. The cold water comes into the house from either a community source or from a private well. The cold water system in your house branches off to distribute water to various fixtures around the house and to the water heater from which the hot water is distributed to many of the same fixtures.

The other system takes the wastewater from the fixture's drains away from the house. The resulting gases must be vented outside of the house, and pressure must be equalized inside the drainpipes to allow efficient drainage. This system is called the drain-waste-vent or DWV. The wastewater leaves your house through a main drain line that is connected to a community sewer line or to your septic tank.

If you are hoping to add a plumbing fixture to the garage, you need to consider making modifications to both systems. We start with the water supply system.

Older homes had galvanized steel pipes installed to distribute both hot and cold water. I actually found lead distribution pipe in the abandoned 1850s-era house we are now renovating. The galvanized steel pipe is joined with threaded connectors and is no longer used in new construction. Fittings and pipe can still be purchased to make repairs.

Transition fittings also can be purchased to allow you to connect more modern materials to the existing system. Those more modern materials are copper and plastic. Here's the first of our building code remarks. Copper is the most widely used material for water supply systems, but plastic pipes are becoming more popular. You need to check with the local building department to find out exactly what is allowed and how to install it.

Making modifications to the DWV system is usually a bit more involved. Most drainpipes in older homes are cast iron. Most building codes now allow the use of plastic pipe for drains. Again, check with the building department to see what is allowed and how to make the transition from your new plastic pipe into the existing cast iron pipe.

The drain line from your new fixture to the main drain line must have the proper slope and most likely must be vented. Drainpipes carrying any kind of waste must have a slope of at least $1/4$ inch per foot, but no more than $1/2$ inch per foot. Too little slope and the wastewater just sits there and doesn't flow to the main drainpipe; too much slope and the water drains too fast, leaving solid waste in the line to possibly form clogs. This can be a tricky part of installing a new drain line. Another tricky part can be running a vent line.

Do you know where the main hot and cold water supply lines are? If you plan to install a utility sink, you might be able to just tie in to the existing lines of a kitchen sink or a bathroom that may have plumbing in a shared wall with the garage. If you are planning on a fixture that needs a greater volume of water, you probably need to move closer to the main branches of your water distribution system before tying in. Do you know where the main drain lines are?

The vertical vent stacks usually will be close to a toilet and terminate above in a penetration through the roof. They connect at the bottom into a main drainpipe. Generally, you cannot add or install multiple fixtures on a smaller drainpipe. If you have a basement or adequate crawlspace, you may find easy access to the drainpipes and supply lines. If your house is built on a slab, your plumbing may be buried in concrete, which doesn't allow easy access. Take your drawings to the local building department or consult with a professional plumber to see how feasible your project will be.

HVAC

Is your garage a two-season garage? Do you find spring and fall okay for working in the garage? Does the blistering heat make your car so hot that you park it outside? Do you rush into the house in the winter? Perhaps your garage would benefit from climate control.

The garage is a more difficult place in which to control the climate. The walls and ceiling may not be insulated, windows and doors probably don't seal as well as the windows and doors in your home, and every time that big door opens there is a significant exchange of air.

Heating, cooling, and ventilation are important considerations for both your comfort and for everything stored in the garage. A climate-controlled garage also provides a more stable environment for the building itself.

Ventilation can be achieved by simply opening a window, setting a fan in a window, or installing and operating a wall or ceiling mounted exhaust fan. If you decide to install an exhaust fan, carefully consider where to locate it to provide maximum efficiency and where ductwork can be run or where the wall vent will be the least obtrusive. The supplier should be able to help you decide which unit will work best for you. You also need to check with your local building department for regulations covering the installation.

If you spend time in your garage during warm weather, you could find some comfort from a strategically placed ceiling fan. There are inexpensive utility styles that function well, and there are installation kits to provide a secure mounting. Your home improvement center should have a decent selection and will be able to offer advice and answer questions. A window air conditioner may be another possibility, or you may even consider mounting the air conditioner in a wall opening if a convenient window is not available.

Heating the garage probably will be the most involved of the climate-control modifications. How it is accomplished depends on many factors. What type of fuel or energy is available? How easy is it to get it or warm air into the garage? These are a few of the questions that have to be answered. A good place to start is your local building department.

Heat sources in a garage, especially an attached garage, will be carefully regulated. You may want to consider one or more wall-mounted space heaters to heat a corner or portion of your garage, while you are out there working on something. Other conventional options include electric baseboard heat or radiant heat. A less-conventional option is to add solar panels to the roof if you live in an area where this is feasible. You may even consider adding a wood-burning stove to the garage. It will require significantly more space than the other options, more protective materials to shield combustible objects, and more maintenance.

Warning Light

Heating systems can be extremely dangerous to work on. Not only is high heat involved, but also very volatile fuels. Electrical service may involve 240 volts.

If you find that the portable heating or air-conditioning in your garage isn't working adequately, consider the next step up, which will be costly. That is installing heating and central air. The climate-control systems in large, new residential construction are sometimes designed with multiple furnaces and air-conditioning units. This allows for greater control. Individual floors may have their own units, or areas, such as the sleeping area, may have dedicated units. The same idea can work for your garage.

This will be a major remodeling undertaking in an existing garage. Careful planning will be essential to provide the most efficient system. Depending on how the system is designed, electricity will need to be provided, perhaps 240 volts, plumbing may be needed, and structural modifications could be necessary. With so much needing to be coordinated, it is wise to get professional HVAC specialists to design a system for you, and then have that system reviewed by the building department to pull the necessary permits.

Codes, Permits, and Deed Restrictions

Building codes are written to protect the health and safety of the occupants of your home, your neighbors, and the future occupants of your home. So although it is easy to understand why there are codes, it sometimes seems like the codes just make it more difficult to make the modifications you want. Keep an open mind

and try to work with your inspector, remembering that his primary concern is safety and not design. The codes also are in force to be sure that areas maintain a certain atmosphere or that properties in an area do not deviate too much from accepted building practices. For example, if you drive into some rural areas, you will see that there are a mix of styles, sizes, and construction techniques there. In newer areas, you may find that codes require a minimum of so many square feet in a house, certain types of exterior finishes, or certain construction techniques, especially in hurricane-, earthquake-, or flood-prone areas. There may be other restrictions, too. Maybe the garage has to be level with your house, or a building on your property has to be so many feet from the next property. This could have an effect on you if you are planning to add some space onto your garage.

You must display your permit in a conspicuous place.

Photo by Theresa Russell

Local building codes from different locations may not agree on what does and does not require a permit. It is always best to ask first, get the permit, and do the work. Don't assume you don't need a permit and start work. Building inspectors can issue stop work orders and require that all modifications be removed. Ignorance is not a viable excuse.

A permit is issued when your plans comply with the local codes. The process can be a very simple matter. You fill out the application, submit your plans, and pay your fees. Or your plans need to be reviewed by senior staff to make sure they comply with all requirements. You may be asked to provide approval and signatures of professional designers, architects, or structural engineers if you haven't already. There may be some back-and-forth discussion, questions to be answered, and design changes to be made before approval. Much depends on the people who work in your code enforcement office. Be nice to them. Once you have your permit, inspections will be required at various times during the construction. Don't do more work than allowed before each inspection, such as closing up walls with drywall before a rough mechanical inspection, or you will most likely be asked to remove it. If you have hired a contractor to do the work, he or she will pull the permits, schedule inspections, and make sure the work is in compliance with the building code.

Housing Associations

You might be able to secure a permit for your work because it will meet code. That does not mean that it will meet the requirements of your housing association. They often have their own rules to keep the neighborhood looking a certain way. Some may require that you park the cars in the garage, or that cars, but not pickup trucks, may be parked on the driveway. Others may not allow any larger items like kayaks or boats to be stored anywhere other than inside the garage, and that includes the backyard. Some may not permit a separate shed. Yet others may require that garage doors be of one design or one color. Don't mess with these people. Some of us would never live in a neighborhood with a housing association just because of the control they have over our real estate.

Historic Designations

If your house is designated a historic building or is part of a historic preservation area, you may have some even more stringent restrictions to deal with. They may dictate the color of your garage as well as any other details of it, especially if it changes the historical integrity of the garage.

Hiring Pros

Many of these upgrades are major and should be left to the pros. A professional does this every day and has seen many garages and situations such as yours. Professionals can quickly see any possible problems and prevent them before they even happen. They may also have alternative suggestions for doing your project. Be open-minded and listen to their suggestions.

If you are planning extensive changes to your garage, you may want to consider hiring a general or remodeling contractor. This contractor's primary responsibility will be the management of both the construction and business aspects of your project. He or she will start with a careful analysis of your plans, will pull all necessary permits and coordinate inspections, will purchase all materials needed, will hire and supervise all specialty subcontractors as needed, and will supervise all work until completion.

You may decide to do some of the work yourself and only need a specialty contractor for specific tasks. The three that we have been concerned with in this chapter are the electrical, the plumbing, and the HVAC contractors. The electrical contractor runs the rough wiring and makes the necessary connections and modifications at the service panel. He then returns, if necessary, to complete his job by installing fixtures, outlets, and switches after other work, such as wall coverings, is completed. The plumbing contractor works in a similar fashion to the electrician. He or she needs to rough in supply lines and drainpipes and then return if necessary to finish the installation of the plumbing fixtures. The HVAC contractor may be even more specialized depending on the type of work you are having done. Some specialize in certain fuel types or certain distribution systems.

You may want to refer back to Chapter 5 for suggestions on hiring the expert help. Make sure to get three quotes. Make sure the contractors are experienced, qualified, and licensed.

The Least You Need to Know

- Know what your abilities are and hire professionals for jobs beyond your skill level.
- Understand the dangers involved when dealing with electricity and fuel.
- Take the time to understand how mechanical systems work.
- Devise a logical and cost-effective plan for upgrading.
- Make sure all your work complies with code and regulations.
- Safety cannot be emphasized often enough.

In This Chapter

- ◆ Understanding how walls are built and modified
- ◆ Installing drywall
- ◆ Choosing a floor finish

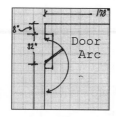

Chapter 17

Upgrading Structure and Finish

Creating that functional garage that you've been dreaming about might involve more than hanging a pegboard or a new coat of paint. Some garage solutions may need a structural improvement to accommodate another improvement you are doing. Maybe your current garage is an older model, was underbuilt, or is just not as functional as you need. You have plenty of options for turning it into the space that you really want.

Just a reminder: before you consider doing this, you need to look at your budget. The labor involved will often be the major portion of the cost. Unless you are skilled in some or any of the construction trades, it is a wise idea to hire experts to do those tasks, especially when it comes to modifying the load-bearing structure of your house or garage.

You also need to check on local building codes, deed restrictions, housing association rules, and the like. Checking into these rules will save a lot of frustration in case you find out that the color of the new garage door doesn't comply with your neighborhood housing association's rules. It is up to you to be sure you are compliant with any local regulations.

Budget Considerations

The previous chapters in the book have helped you determine what you need, what will work for you, and whether you can and will install the solution. After you finalized your design, you may have found that some significant structural modifications need to be made or extensive new finishes need to be applied.

As in Chapter 16, the same guidelines and suggestions for cost estimates and budgeting apply to structural projects as they did to mechanical modifications. Refer back to the first section in Chapter 16 for details on the breakdown of labor and material costs and on preparing to obtain estimates for your project.

Structural Improvements and Reinforcements

Whatever the scope of the work you need done, it helps to know some basics about the structural components that hold your home and garage upright and together. This way you can make an informed decision if you decide to do some of the work yourself or you can better understand what the contractor is doing.

Construction 101

We start from the bottom and work our way up. Your foundation, which is most likely made from poured concrete or concrete block, distributes the weight of your entire home, its contents, and you and your family over the land on which it rests. Foundation work requires some muscle (concrete is heavy and strong), some specialized equipment, especially for cutting and boring, and some expertise whether for modifying an existing structure or laying up new block. These jobs are best left to the experts.

On top of the foundation is the floor, concrete in your garage and either wooden framed or concrete slab in your house. Producing the flat, smooth, level surface of your garage floor requires more of that expertise.

The walls in your garage sit on top of the floor or an extension of the foundation. The walls are constructed of horizontal components, called plates, and vertical components, called studs. When studs are missing for openings, such as doors and windows, headers are installed to distribute the weight that would have been carried by the missing studs to other studs.

The exterior walls typically carry the weight of the ceilings and the roof. These walls and any other walls that contribute to the support of the house structure are considered *load-bearing walls*. Walls that serve only as partitions and support only themselves are considered *non-load-bearing walls*.

Definitions

A **load-bearing wall** is a wall that supports the weight of the house. Remove this wall and the house could collapse.

A **non-load-bearing wall** is a wall that does not support any structural components other than itself. Remove this wall and there would be no structural damage.

Warning Light

Determining whether a particular wall is load-bearing is not always easy. Perimeter walls are typically load-bearing and certain interior walls will also be load-bearing. Ask an expert, such as a contractor or building inspector, for an expert opinion before attempting to modify a wall.

Ceilings are framed with horizontal beams called joists that rest atop the walls. The final component is the roof frame made up of rafters that also are supported by the walls.

Drive It Home

If you had a framing contractor modify some walls for windows or doors and you are going to complete the work by installing the windows or doors, check the rough opening size and make sure it corresponds to the requirements of your new window or door. Manufacturers' instructions will vary. Follow the instructions specific to this product to ensure a proper installation and a trouble-free future.

Ceilings and Walls

You probably will not be concerned with modifying ceilings or roofs. If you do need to make those modifications, consult a framing contractor and, at the very least, discuss your potential alterations with your local building inspector.

Your primary concern probably will be with walls—specifically with removing, modifying, replacing, or installing one where none existed previously. Removing a garage wall can be tricky (so can modifying one because it is likely that all the walls in a garage could be load-bearing). Consult the experts before proceeding. Installing a new wall is normally done in one of two ways.

The first technique requires that you:

1. Mark stud locations on the top and bottom plates every 16 inches on center.
2. Secure the bottom plate to the floor using concrete fasteners.
3. Attach the top plate to the ceiling with fasteners driven into the ceiling joists.

4. Measure the distance between the top and bottom plates at each stud location. Since the garage floor may slope and the ceiling may be level, the distances could vary at each location.
5. Cut the studs to length.
6. Insert each stud at the marked location and secure by toe nailing.

Suppose you have plenty of room on the garage floor; then you could use technique number two. You will:

1. Mark stud locations on the top and bottom plates every 16 inches on center.
2. Measure the distance between the floor and the ceiling at 16-inch intervals where your wall will be placed.
3. Subtract 3 1/4 inches from each measurement and cut a stud to length for each of those measurements.
4. Lay the top and bottom plates on edge about a stud length apart with the stud markings facing each other.
5. Place a corresponding stud between the plates at each of the stud markings.
6. Secure each stud by nailing through the plates.
7. Tilt the finished wall frame into place.
8. Plumb the wall and secure the bottom plate with concrete fasteners and secure the top plate with fasteners into each of the ceiling joists.

Warning Light

If you build your wall outside, keep in mind the garage door is lower than the ceiling. Depending on the height of your ceiling, you may have to tilt the wall to get it into the garage. Then simply lift in place. For smaller doors with higher ceilings, build the wall in two sections.

After your walls are secured in place, electrical lines and fixture boxes can be roughed in along with any plumbing or ductwork. Install insulation if needed, and now you can hang your wall covering. Remember to have all necessary inspections done before insulating and closing the wall. The inspections include, but are not necessarily limited to, framing, plumbing, electrical, ductwork, and insulation.

Drywall

Drywall is the most common wall covering. There are a variety of types, including regular, moisture resistant, fire code, and dent resistant. It is comparatively inexpensive, easy to cut and hang, and has reasonably easy techniques to finish joints. Drywall typically measures four feet wide, but comes in a variety of thicknesses ($^3/_8$, $^1/_2$, and $^5/_8$ inches) and lengths (8, 10, 12 and 16 feet). 4'×8' sheets of $^1/_2$" drywall are the most common. Check with your local building department to see which type is allowed in your application and what type of fastener must be used. Some codes will also dictate where and how many fasteners must be used.

Loose Change

After having hung countless ceilings with drywall using crude supports and helpers, I rented a drywall hoist. For about $35 a day, it made a difficult, tedious job into a fairly easy one-man operation. It saved time and backs. A hoist is on my short list of tools to buy.

A drywall hoist made installing a ceiling much easier in less time and with much less stress on our backs.

Photo by Theresa Russell

Installing drywall is not too difficult. Listed here are the basic steps:

1. Install ceiling drywall first, using drywall nails or screws at the specified intervals.

2. If necessary, cut the sheet to size using a drywall square and a utility knife. You simply score one side along the edge of the square, bend the sheet at the score until it snaps, and then cut through the paper at the crease.

3. Place the drywall sheet against the studs or joists and nail or screw into place at the specified intervals, making sure you have penetrated the wood with each fastener.

4. Continue placing sheet edges firmly against each other, matching long edges to long edges and short edges to short edges. Plan so that the ends of the sheet always fall on a stud or joist.

5. Apply a bed of joint compound in the tapered joint along the long edges and press paper drywall tape into the compound. Smooth it out and remove any excess compound. Next, repeat the process on any joints formed by the nontapered short edges. Try to use enough compound to embed the tape, but minimize the joint rising above the plane of the drywall surface.

6. After the compound has dried, sand or scrape off any high spots and, using a wider drywall knife, apply a second coat covering the tape.

7. After this coat has dried, apply a thin final coat using a still wider drywall knife.

8. When this coat is dry, sand lightly, prime, and paint.

A variety of products are variations on a theme. Visit your home improvement center and you will find self-adhesive tape that eliminates one of the coats; special metal, vinyl, and combination products for inside and outside corners; and several types of joint compound.

Other Finishes

Although drywall is by far the most popular wall covering, there are other options to consider. Check your local building code to make sure what you want is in compliance. Perhaps a wall or all walls covered completely in pegboard or slat wall would be very useful. We discussed how exterior wall covering could be used on the inside of a garage in Chapter 10. Visit your home improvement center to see what's readily available.

Flooring

Concrete is the material of choice for garage floors. It is relatively inexpensive, quite strong, and generally practical. For parking the car, it's great. For most other uses, it leaves something to be desired. Bare concrete does not clean particularly well, and it is prone to staining. It is a hard, unforgiving surface that can be detrimental to some objects placed on it, and standing on it for long periods of time results in stress and fatigue for the back and feet.

Finishes

Painting is the most common way to finish a concrete floor. It is also the quickest and least-expensive way to improve your floor. There is a broad range of prices and several different types of floor paint available. Success or peeling depends on two factors.

First, is there moisture present in the concrete? Test by taping a piece of plastic sheeting about 1 foot by 1 foot to the floor on all edges to seal it completely. Wait 24 to 48 hours and see whether water collected on the sheet or if the concrete was darkened by moisture permeating from below. If you detect moisture, use a product that specifically addresses this problem.

The second factor is the preparation. Is there paint, sealer, or clear coating on the floor? Is it peeling? For proper adhesion on a dry floor, you may need to wash, chemical strip, etch with acid, or mechanically strip and abrade the surface. Then a primer may need to be applied before the final coat. A variety of paints and coatings, including concrete floor paint, acrylic epoxies, and two-part epoxies, have specific preparation requirements.

Loose Change

We check for mismatched paint whenever we are in the store. The price is reasonable and there is usually just about any type of paint that you need. We mix colors together to create our own color. Alternatively, you can grab the reduced can of a color you like and have more paint mixed to match it.

Other kinds of coatings include thin cement-based coatings (which can be textured to resemble a variety of surfaces) and true or imitation terrazzo floors.

Other Materials

Carpet is always an option, especially if you are not parking the car in the garage. Use two-sided carpet tape to secure it rather than gluing it down, making it easier to replace or remove if you decide to park the car in the garage during the winter. You may want to consider self-stick carpet tiles designed for garages. They come in larger sizes than standard carpet tiles and can be removed and repositioned.

Commercial floor tile also works well in a garage. Several new floor products might be just right for you. Wide sheets of heavy durable plastic (either smooth or with embossed designs) are specifically designed for use in garages. Large interlocking plastic tiles are also available.

You also could build a floor covering from wood using some of the moisture-resistant engineered panels or using some of the interlocking subfloor tiles designed for finishing basement floors. The best advice for installing any of these products is to carefully and completely follow the manufacturer's instructions.

You need not limit yourself to using only one type of floor covering. You could use different materials to define specific areas or apply different coverings for heavy or light use. We heard of a garage floor covered with tile around the raised perimeter so that an area rug could be used in the recessed area when entertaining in the garage. When the party is over, roll up the rug and you once again have the parking space for the car.

Garage Doors

The garage door is the biggest entry into your house. It makes quite a statement from the curb if your garage is front-loading. Any changes to the door can significantly improve the appearance of your house. If your door is more than 10 years old, it probably should be replaced for safety reasons, unless it has been upgraded to conform to the latest safety requirements.

Photo by Jeld-Wen

Photo by Overhead

Photo by Overhead

Photo by Clopay

Photo by Clopay

Photo by Overhead

Garage doors come in many styles and materials.

You can go with a generic, utility-type door and paint it to blend in unobtrusively with the rest of the exterior of your home. Or you can find a door that matches, even highlights, the architectural style of your house and makes a dramatic statement.

Drive It Home

Trying to install two smaller garage doors in place of one large one can be a significant and expensive structural modification. You may want to consider changing the garage door to achieve this effect.

You can buy a single door that looks like two doors.

Photo by Overhead

An insulated door offers potential energy savings in heating and cooling costs. Look for a wind-loaded system door if you live in a hurricane area.

It is best to have a professional install the garage door and the garage door opener (because there are several fairly involved adjustments) to ensure safe and easy operation.

A wind-loaded door would be a better choice.

Photo by Clopay

Get to Know Your Garage Door

Now that you have seen what a difference a garage door can make in a house, you need to familiarize yourself with your garage door and its parts. Refer to the illustration and basic terms here.

Garage Door Safety

A garage door is probably the largest and heaviest moving part of your home. There are three safety features that should be tested regularly:

◆ The safety reverse beam should be installed 4 to 6 inches off the floor. When the beam is broken, the direction of the door should reverse.

◆ The auto-reverse sensor should reverse the direction of the door either when an object is encountered in the path of the door or when the door encounters moderate resistance in either direction.

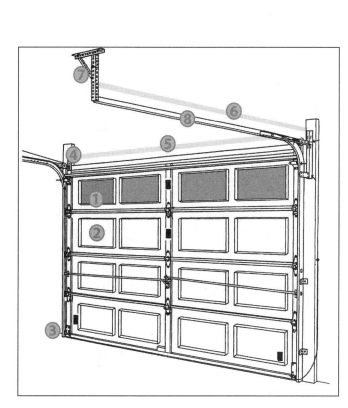

1. Window Lite
Glazed section with various types of glass or clear acrylic to allow for light and visibility.

2. Sections
Steel panels reinforced with stiles interconnected with hinges and rollers.

3. Bottom Bracket
A structured support, which provides for attachment of lifting cables.

4. Cable Drum
Grooved drums on the torsion spring shaft that lifting cables wind around when door is opening.

5. Torsion Springs
Provides the means to raise and lower the garage door via cable winding on drums.

6. Extension
Extend along both horizontal tracks.

7. Rear Track Hanger

8. Track
Provides a guide for section to raise or lower the garage door.

Track Types:
Standard
Low Headroom

Track Components:
Vertical Track: on either side of opening.
Horizontal Track: attached to ceiling.
Radius: curved track

Standard Heights:
7 feet high–4 sections high
8 feet high–5 sections high

Gauge = thickness of steel
Lower is better. 24 gauge is thicker than 25 gauge.

Photo by Clopay

◆ The last safety feature is the safety counter balance spring. With the door in the closed position, disconnect the opener by tripping the release mechanism. You should be able to open the door with little effort, and it should remain balanced at the half-open position.

Warning Light _____

Garage door maintenance and safety testing is one of the most commonly neglected tasks of homeowners. Photoelectric eyes have been required since 1993, reversing mechanisms have been required since 1991, and emergency disconnects became standard in 1982. The Consumer Product Safety Commission recommends a monthly testing of the safety systems.

Problems with the first two tests may be corrected by adjustments detailed in the owner's manual or by the replacement of an older unit. If your door fails the third test, the balance tension should be adjusted only by a qualified service professional. The balance springs are under significant tension and can cause serious injury during adjustment.

Garage door openers must now have all of these safety features. Professional garage door installers, service people, and retailers are not allowed to install, service, repair, or sell any openers that do not meet UL325 Federal Safety Standards.

A properly installed and regularly maintained garage door can provide many years of safe and dependable service. Here is a list of some suggestions to ensure those years of safe and trouble-free service:

◆ Conduct monthly safety checks and provide the regular maintenance as outlined in your owner's manual. Schedule an annual inspection and service call from a professional garage door specialist.

◆ Keep the owner's manual for the garage door and for the opener close by for quick and easy reference during the safety checks or to resolve any problem.

◆ Have frayed cables or broken springs replaced. Always replace them in pairs, even if only one is worn or broken. Do not attempt to do this on your own. The cables and springs are under great tension, and can cause serious injury when they break or come loose. Always have this work done by a trained professional.

◆ Your door should go up and down easily without unusual noises. If it doesn't or you hear squeaks, grinding, and groans, you could have an unsafe situation or maybe just a needed minor adjustment. Do not continue operating the door under these conditions. Have the problem evaluated and resolved by a trained professional.

◆ Always use the lift handles when opening and closing the door manually. Never open and close the door by grabbing a corner or grabbing in between sections.

◆ If your garage door has extension springs, make sure the containment cables are securely fastened at each end. If the cables are missing or loose, reinstall them.

◆ If you want to do some or all of the work involved in installation, replacement, or upgrading of the garage door or opener, be aware of all the hazards involved and the potential for serious or fatal injury. Read and reread the manufacturer's instructions, use the correct tools, follow the recommended procedures precisely, and keep safety a priority.

Improve Energy Efficiency

A project that most do-it-yourselfers can do is improving the energy efficiency of a noninsulated or leaky insulated door. Several insulation kits are available. The bottom weather strip is a common replacement item that can minimize weather leakage. There are also several versions of perimeter seals that are applied to the doorjambs and header to keep wind, dust, rain, and snow out of the garage.

Hiring Pros

You may want to consider hiring a general contractor if you are planning extensive structural changes to your garage, or you may decide to do some of the work yourself and only need a specialty contractor for specific tasks. Some of the specialty contractors you may need are listed here:

◆ An excavation contractor will dig, backfill, and grade an area where a foundation is being installed or modified. A foundation contractor will set up forms, lay block, and coordinate with other tradespeople about

burying mechanicals in the concrete. The concrete contractor will pour and finish concrete. Many contractors will do all three of these jobs, often maintaining separate crews for each task.

◆ A framing contractor will build a new wall or modify the structural elements of an existing one. He or she will build or modify any of the other structural components of the framework in your home or garage. Some of these contractors may specialize in door and window installations.

◆ Drywall contractors often maintain separate crews for hanging and finishing drywall. Some even have a painting crew, or you could hire your own painting contractor.

The Least You Need to Know

◆ The structural framework of your garage supports the walls, ceiling, and roof.

◆ Before removing or modifying a wall, determine whether it is load-bearing and then act accordingly.

◆ Regular safety maintenance on your garage door will not only keep you and your family safe, but will also extend its life.

◆ Always schedule building inspections to coincide with each step of your work as it is completed and needs to be checked.

In This Chapter

◆ Motivation to keep the garage clean

◆ Regularly maintain your system and garage

◆ Reevaluate your solutions

◆ Dealing with seasonal storage

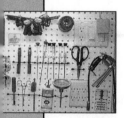

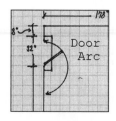

Chapter 18

Keep It Organized

Don't let all those hours of time you spent getting your garage perfect fall by the wayside. You don't really want to go through this again, do you? Look at how clean and functional your garage is right now. Isn't that nice?

Wouldn't it be great if it always looked like this? You can do a few things to keep it from reverting to its former state.

The key is to regularly attend to it. Don't neglect it. Don't throw something in there with the intent of putting it in its place later. That one thing you toss in there will eventually be joined by a lot of other things that you will get to later. The garage won't stay in this condition by itself. You need to help it along. It won't always be easy, but occasionally you need to do a few things to keep it looking good. It isn't too early to start a new habit.

Regular Maintenance

Time is always an issue with the hectic lives we lead today. Who has time to scrape off the peeling paint or to clean the oil leak on the floor when it happens? The key here is to get into the routine of immediately following up with any spills, dirt, or repair.

For some of us, that is no problem. For the rest of us, getting into a new routine can be difficult.

Drive It Home

Diane offers these tips for maintaining your garage space:

Continue to "contain to maintain"—contain new "stuff" introduced into your storage space until you have time to integrate it into the system. Plan to use the last 10 minutes of every hour to "clean up" if you are doing projects in your newly organized space. Quit working half an hour before you must so that you can put everything away in its home. Set aside some time each week to "tweak" your storage areas.

Keep in mind that you have already done the hard part of the job. You need to give the same importance to this room as you would to any other room in the house. Pay attention to it just as you would the rest of your house. Spend just 5 or 10 minutes every day doing a clean sweep of the area. This will prevent things from piling back up. If you don't have time to commit to the garage on a daily basis, set aside an hour or so every weekend to clean, reorganize, and find places for the additional things you have relegated to the garage.

Think about when you were sorting those piles to get rid of stuff. Do that again with the new things you have put into the garage. Should you keep or get rid of what you just put in your garage? If it is something you really should get rid of, take action immediately. Call a charity, list it on eBay, or post it on Sharing Is Giving.

If you do decide to keep something, first be sure the garage is the best place to store it. Remember how the garage seems to become the catchall storage space for everything? Get out of this mind-set. There may be a better place in the house to keep something. Don't fall back into old habits.

Some maintenance fits better into a monthly schedule. Maintaining the outside of your garage fits into this rotation. Repair anything as it happens. You don't need to worry about water from a leaky roof getting into your garage. Watch for any spots where insects or rodents might be trying to get in. Attend to this immediately.

You don't want your garage to go back to this, do you?

Photo by Rand Ruland

Keep your space looking like this.

Photo by ClosetMaid

Your new system will only work for you if you maintain it. If you moved your office into the garage, treat it just as you would if it were inside the house. Replace light bulbs as needed. Replace the label that fell off one of your bins. If you had a bin of something that you couldn't decide whether to keep or not, go look in it and see if you can make a decision now. If you haven't used whatever is in it, maybe it is time to get rid of it. Are there any other parts of your new system that need repairs? Has a handle fallen off a drawer? Do you need to tighten any screws? Many things become loose over time.

Do your regular garage door safety check. This is especially important if you have children. When you do your door check, also check your smoke detector and carbon monoxide tester batteries.

Be sure to do routine garage door safety inspections.

Photo by Wesson Garage

Warning Light

Be sure to do a monthly garage door safety inspection. The safety features added to new garage doors has contributed to a decrease in accidents and fatalities. Do your part to keep your garage a safe place.

Don't get frustrated if you do find yourself falling back into your old habits. Take a deep breath. Think about what you are doing. Remember that it takes 21 repetitions to form a new habit. Plan on three weeks to transform yourself and adopt this new habit.

> **$ Loose Change**
>
> If you are having trouble keeping your space clean and can't afford to hire somebody, think about getting a buddy to help you. If your buddy helps you reorganize, you can help him do the same at his garage. Often having a buddy keeps you on track.

If you have real difficulties, hire somebody to clean the garage on a regular basis. If that isn't a possibility, join a support group. Yes, there are such online groups out there, so you don't even need to leave home for support. Two such groups are Messies Anonymous and Squalor Survivors.

Reevaluation of Function

After you have been using your system for a while, you need to reevaluate how it is working for you. If things are going smoothly, don't change anything. If you find that you are still spending too much time looking for things, you need to make some changes. The changes don't need to be drastic. It could be a simple matter of relabeling something. If you are always trying to remember what exactly is in a bin with a certain label, you need a more descriptive label for that bin. You might want to make a label that lists everything in the bin. This will save you time and frustration. If you still need to spend a lot of time opening bins or going through toolboxes, you need to tweak your system.

How does your garage compare?
Photo by Schulte

Consider the components of your system. Maybe you thought that one certain product would be absolutely perfect for your need. However, after using it, you decided that something simpler or smaller would do the job, too. Perhaps you just hate how something looks in a certain place. Move it. Replace it. Or use it for a different purpose. There is absolutely nothing wrong with changing your plan. The goal is to make it efficient and functional.

Keep looking for new ideas or new products that might make life easier for you. It is possible that when you were searching for the perfect product, it was not available. Garage organization has become a major part of the home improvement market. New things come on the market all the time, so that bin in the right size and the right color may be out there now.

There are plenty of storage products on the market.

Photo by Rand Ruland

Give any new arrangement or product a little while to earn its keep. If things seem to be working well, stick with this arrangement. If you still have some problems with the system, keep tweaking until you get it right.

Seasonal Influences

Your garage is a dynamic storage space. Often things move around a lot. Many things go in and out of the your garage. Others get moved inside and outside the garage. Yard equipment is one such category. In the summer, the kiddie pool goes outside. If you have a larger pool, the equipment that you stored throughout the winter moves outside. Ideally, you will have a special area for things that need to be moved on a regular basis. For seasonal items that get moved at the beginning and end of the season, you might consider storing them in a less-than-ideal place because you don't need to have access to them on a regular basis.

Drive It Home

Store your seasonal items in color-coded bins. Use a different color for each season.

If you store your grill in the garage, you certainly want to have easy access to it on a daily basis throughout the grilling season. If you don't grill in the winter, its place might change during those months. You might rotate it with other seasonal items that are used in the opposite time of the year.

Some of the things in your garage might stay outside the entire summer. This might free up some space that you could use for something else. Maybe that space lends itself to setting up a summer craft area for the kids. Keep your options open.

Be sure that you change around the location of your seasonal items before you need them. Don't wait until the middle of winter to pull out the sleds or ice skates. Put away the summer stuff and move it out of the way. Bring the winter stuff up to the front or into an area that is easily accessible.

Don't mix your seasonal items in one container. You don't want to sort through the Fourth of July decorations to find your favorite Christmas tree ornament.

You may do more than use your garage to store different seasonal item. When the warm weather comes, you might transform your garage into a recreation room or a screened-in summer room. That means installing a screen on the door, setting out the furniture, and moving the car out of the garage for the summer. The garage might be the perfect spot for the kids to play on rainy days.

You might want to use your garage as an extra room in the summer.

Photo by GarageTek

Photo by Schulte

Photo by Schulte

Photo by Erik Russell

Photo by ClosetMaid

**Keep your garage
looking like these.**

Whether you use your garage for storage, for the car, or for an extra summer room, you need to maintain it. Keeping a regular routine will keep your garage in tip-top shape. It will keep you sane, too.

The Least You Need to Know

◆ Build and maintain good organizational habits.

◆ Maintenance promotes order and safety.

◆ Be flexible and willing to change your garage.

◆ Enjoy your new and improved garage.

Glossary

10d nail   Nails are measured by their lengths using either inches or pennies. The penny is designated by the letter *d*. The 2d nail measures in at 1 inch. For each additional *d*, you should add ¼" to the length. So a 10d nail will be 3" long. The system changes for anything bigger than a 10d nail. This system originated centuries ago and was probably based on the cost of 100 nails.

access hole   An opening in a floor, wall, or ceiling that provides access to the space between the studs or joists or to an attic or crawl space.

amperage   The movement of the electrical current in a circuit, measured in amps.

bit   An attachment for drills. These bits may drive screws or bore holes.

carriage house   The spot to park the horse and buggy. With the advent of the car, the garage came into being, and the carriage house often became a storage place.

caster   One of a set of wheels attached to the bottom of cabinets or toolboxes to provide mobility.

ceiling plan   A representation of what you would see if you were lying on the floor looking up.

chattel   A piece of property that is not real estate. An aboveground pool or wheelbarrow is a chattel.

circuit   A continuous path of electrical current flowing through wires from a power source to a fixture and back to the source.

circuit breaker A safety switch that interrupts the flow of current through a circuit in the event of a short or overload.

code A basic set of requirements to ensure safety and structural integrity of buildings and mechanical systems. It ensures that systems meet minimum requirements.

conduit A rigid covering that protects electrical wires.

Consumer Product Safety Commission An organization that rates and recommends safety performance of products.

creeper A rolling platform used to easily access the underside of a car.

dead load The weight of the permanent components of a building structure that must be supported by the structure.

deed restriction A clause written into your deed that dictates the use of your property in a certain way. It can also restrict certain chattels or activities on your property. For instance, you might not be allowed to have an aboveground pool or a clothesline in your backyard.

dolly A four-wheeled platform to move heavy objects.

drain-waste-vent (DWV) The plumbing system that removes wastewater from your home and vents odors and gases to the outside.

drywall Also called gypsum board, Sheetrock, gyp-board, or wallboard. Drywall consists of flat sheets of gypsum sandwiched between heavy paper. The long edges of the sheets, which are usually 4'×8' or 4'×12' have tapered edges where joint compound and tape are applied to hide the seams. It comes in regular, moisture-resistant, and fire grades. Thicknesses vary, too.

efflorescence A white, powdery substance caused by water leaking through a solid surface like concrete, brick, or tile. It is caused by the residual salts from the water as it passes through to the surface.

electrical Wiring outside of walls, conduit, service panels, lights, switches, and receptacles.

enamel A type of paint that dries leaving a durable, hard, glossy finish.

engineered joists Beams manufactured from wood products using glues and resins to create uniform, stable, and predictable structural components.

fascia The vertical trim that covers the ends of the rafters.

feng shui The Chinese art of placement.

fire rating The amount of time it takes to burn through a surface.

flashing Sheet metal used to reinforce and weatherproof the joints and angles of a roof.

floor plan The floor plan is the horizontal view of your space. Think about what you would see if you were looking down from the ceiling.

fuse A safety device that interrupts the flow of current through a circuit in the event of a short or overload.

gauge The size of the wire; the smaller the number, the larger the wire diameter and the more current it will carry.

general contractor Supervises all aspects of work done at the job site. Hires and pays the subcontractors, coordinates permits and inspections, and purchases all materials.

glazing The glass in a window. Double-glazed windows have two layers of glass.

gloss The amount of sheen the final paint finish will have.

GFI Ground fault interrupter, a safety switch that quickly stops the flow of current in a circuit that has a shock hazard.

ground Anything such as wiring that conducts current to the earth in the event of a short circuit.

gypsum board *See* drywall.

hand truck A wheeled device for moving heavy objects

HEPA filter High-efficiency particulate air filters are considered the ultimate filters. They trap particles as small as .3 microns with an efficiency of 99.97 percent. This is the dust mask to wear when cleaning. These filters also work in vacuum cleaners and furnaces.

HHW Household hazardous waste. Look for the words "caution," "poison," or "danger" on the label. The major categories of HHWs are those that are flammable or combustible, explosive or reactive, corrosive or toxic.

hot Anything such as wiring that carries voltage.

hot tire pick-up Tires become warm and even hot from friction caused by contact with the road. Tires can become hot enough, especially in the summer, to soften the paint on your garage floor so much that it actually peels off.

housing association A board that regulates exterior improvements, additions, and chattels within the neighborhood.

HVAC The Heating, Ventilation and Air Conditioning system includes furnaces, cooling and condensing units, humidifiers and dehumidifiers, ductwork, and air filtration units.

joist One of a series of parallel beams used to carry floor and ceiling loads. Joists are supported by bearing walls or girders.

keyhole saw A narrow-profile saw used for starting and cutting holes into drywall or other material.

laminate A thin, durable covering over a substrate.

latex Uses a water-based vehicle to carry the pigment and solids that produce the skin or coating.

level A tool used to determine whether surfaces are plumb, level, or at a 45-degree angle.

line terminals The terminals on a receptacle that are connected to the part of the circuit coming directly from the service panel.

live load The weight of people, furniture, and any other items that occupy a building.

load terminals The terminals on a receptacle that are connected to the part of the circuit not coming from the service panel, but the part with the remaining receptacles and fixtures on the circuit.

load-bearing wall A wall that supports the weight of the house. Remove this wall and the house could collapse.

MDF Medium-density fiberboard is a type of hardboard produced by gluing uniformly processed wood fibers under heat and pressure.

mechanicals There are three basic types of mechanicals: plumbing system; electrical system; and heating, cooling, and ventilation system.

NAPO The National Association of Professional Organizers is an organization of professional organizers who enhance the lives of clients by designing systems and processes using organizing principles and through transferring organizing skills.

NEC The National Electrical Code contains specific rules and regulations for practical safeguarding of persons and property from hazards arising from the use of electricity.

neutral Anything such as wiring that returns current to its source at zero voltage.

NM Nonmetallic, usually a thin but very durable plastic.

non-load-bearing wall A wall that does not support any structural components other than itself. Remove this wall and there would be no structural damage.

nuisance abatement When you violate a deed restriction or another ordinance, you are considered a nuisance. The authorities will ask you to correct your problem, which could be removing a nonrunning vehicle or boat from your driveway, for example.

oil Uses a solvent or oil-based vehicle to carry the pigment and solids that produce the skin or coating.

on center The distance between two structural members, measured from the center of one to the center of the adjacent one.

OSB Oriented strand board is constructed by gluing rectangular strands of hardwood or softwood laid up in layers at right angles to each other.

permit A document that gives a homeowner permission to do work. It is usually issued after plans that meet code have been submitted and approved.

plywood The first engineered wood product constructed of gluing thin sheets or veneers of wood with the grain running at right angles.

porte cochère Originally a covered driveway for carriages, it protected passengers from the elements. Some older homes still have this feature. Today, think of the covered area on funeral homes or the drive-thru at the bank.

professional organizer According to the National Association of Professional Organizers (NAPO), "A professional organizer enhances the lives of clients by designing systems and processes using organizing principles and through transferring organizing skills. A professional organizer also educates the public on organizing solutions and the resulting benefits."

PVC Polyvinyl chloride. A plastic used in a variety of building products, such as plumbing pipe, windows, and siding.

rafter One of a series of parallel beams that support a roof system.

resistance The opposition to the flow of current in a circuit, measured in ohms.

return wall The wall that shares the garage door opening.

sheathing Any type of wall covering used on the exterior or on the interior of a house. Frequently refers to exterior grade sheets of plywood.

Sheetrock *See* drywall.

soffit The horizontal covering of the rafter extensions that form the eave.

stud A vertical support made of wood or metal. Usually a 2×4, but larger or smaller in certain applications. They are usually spaced 16 to 24 inches apart from each other.

T-111 A board-and-batten style of finished sheet good that may be of plywood or composite construction. It comes in various thicknesses with various groove spacing and various textures.

TSP Trisodium phosphate is the cleaner of choice for prepping walls for painting. Mixed with a bit of bleach, it will also remove mildew from walls. Wear eye protection and gloves when using it. Don't get it on metal or wood surfaces; it can damage them. Follow the manufacturer's instructions when using this potent cleaner.

vent line   In plumbing, a pipe in the DWV system that allows air to enter and exit the system so that gases can escape and pressure can be equalized.

VOC   Volatile organic compounds are emitted gases from certain solid and nonsolid compounds. Often they are found in cleaning and other everyday products. Some examples include paint, building materials, pesticides, permanent markers, and correction fluid. They may have both short- and long-term adverse effects on your health. Some VOCs are known or suspected carcinogens.

voltage   The electrical force or pressure, measured in volts, that causes current to flow in a circuit.

wall elevation   The vertical view of your space. Think about what you would see if you were standing in front of the walls.

wallboard   *See* drywall.

water   Water heater, water softener, supply lines, drain line, and laundry hookups.

wattage   The power used by an electrical device, measured in watts and calculated by multiplying volts times amps.

Appendix B

Online Resources

This appendix provides a list of online resources to help you declutter your life and organize your garage. There are a plethora of online sites that can help you. Just plug in whatever you are looking for and you will get an overwhelming number of hits on the topic. Here are a few to get you started.

www.diynetwork.com

Organize your garage using tips from this popular resource.

www.garage-ology.com

Garage-ology is the study of garage improvement.

www.garageorganizers.info

Garage organizers provide a variety of organizing tips.

www.housekeeping.about.com

This site has plenty of tips for organizing and storage.

www.overhall.com

Overhaul your life and space with all-encompassing suggestions for how to live and the space you live in.

www.realsimple.com

Real Simple magazine provides tips for cutting the clutter.

www.ronhazelton.com

Ron Hazelton gives commonsense solutions to everyday storage problems.

www.thisoldhouse.com

The popular PBS television program *This Old House* is especially helpful in solving problems that owners of older homes encounter.

Books and Magazines

Books

Fine Homebuilding Editors. *Garage Solutions.* Taunton, 2005.

Gross, Laura. *IdeaWise Garages: Inspiration & Information for Do-It-Yourselfers.* Creative Publishing International, Inc, 2004

Huber, Jeanne. *The Ultimate Garage.* Sunset Publishing Corporation, 2005.

Izsak, Barry. *Organize Your Garage in No Time.* Que Publishing, 2005.

West, Bill. *Your Garagenous Zone: Innovative Ideas for the Garage.* Paragon Garage Company, Ltd., 2004.

Magazines

Better Homes and Gardens, 2006, *Dream Storage Magazine*
Meredith Corporation
125 Park Avenue
New York, NY 10017-5529
212-557-6600
www.bhg.com

Workbench (Tim Robertson, editor)
August Home Publishing Company
2200 Grand Avenue
Des Moines, IA 50312
515-282-7000
www.workbenchmagazine.com

Family Handyman (Ken Collier, editor-in-chief)
RD Publications, Inc.
2915 Commers Drive, Suite 700
Eagan, MN 55121
www.familyhandyman.com

Home (Donna Sapolin, editor-in-chief)
Hachette Magazines, Inc.
1633 Broadway
New York, NY 10019
www.homemag.com

Smart Homeowner
Navigator Publishing LLC (Tim Queeney,
Executive Editor) Bob Feeman is the editor and
he writes the editor letter in the magazine.
58 Fore Street
Portland, ME 04101
207-772-2466
www.SmartHomeOwnerMag.com

Products, Garage Organizers, and Associations

Products

Many of these manufacturers sell their products through franchises, hardware, and home improvement stores or discount stores. They are not always open to the public. Call them or visit their websites to find a location near you that sells the products.

Schulte
12115 Ellington Court
Cincinnati, OH 45249-1000
513-489-9300
www.schultestorage.com

Hyloft
5175 W. Diablo Drive, Suite 110
Las Vegas, NV 89118
702-254-6900, 800-990-6003
www.hyloft.com

Sauder
Archbold, OH
1-800-523-3987
www.sauder.com

JNK
1111 S. 7th Street
Grand Junction, CO 81501
877-873-3736
www.jnkproducts.co

Onwall Solutions
Toronto, Ontario, Canada
877-4-ONWALL, 905-882-1060
www.onwallsolutions.com

Clopay Building Products
8585 Duke Boulevard
Mason, OH 45040-3101
1-800-225-6729
www.clopaydoor.com

Gorgeous Garages
208-356-8820
www.gorgeousgarage.com

TAG, Inc (The Accessories Group)
866-404-8570
www.theaccessoriesgroup.com

ClosetMaid
www.closetmaid.com

GarageTek
5 Aerial Way, Suite 200
Syosset, NY 11791
866-664-2724
www.garagetek.com

diamondLife Gear
Gupta Permold Corporation
234 Lott Road
Pittsburgh, PA 15235
412-793-3511 ext. 104
www.diamondlifegear.com

AlligatorBoard
325 Windy Point Drive
Glendale Heights, IL 60139
866-338-8000
www.alligatorboard.com

Bunjipeg
3512 Carlton Square Place
Raleigh, NC 27612
919-571-1283 ext. 3512
www.bunjipeg.com

Gladiator Garageworks
www.gladiatorgw.com

Riverside Cartop Carriers, Inc.
181 Hill Street
Portsmouth, NH 03801
800-292-2904
www.riversidecartop.com

Better Life Technology, LLC (garage flooring)
9812 Pflumm Road
Lenexa, KS 66215
913-894-0403
www.bltllc.com

Garage Door Screens
55648 Silver Creek Lane
Macomb Twp., MI 48042
810-397-0301
www.garagedoorscreens.com

Jeld-Wen
800-JELD-WEN (800-535-3936)
www.jeld-wen.com

The ADDAHOOK Company
McKinney, TX
214-642-2941
www.addahook.com

O'Sullivan Industries (Coleman)
10 Mansell Court East, Suite 100
Roswell, GA 30076
678-939-0828
www.osullivan.com

Overhead Door
1-800-929-DOOR
www.overheaddoor.com

Yakima Products, Inc.
15025 SW Koll Parkway
Beaverton, OR 90006-6056
971-245-7500
www.yakima.com

Smithy Co.
170 Aprill Drive
P.O. Box 1517
Ann Arbor, MI 48106-1517
800-476-4849
www.smithy.com

Wesson Builders
1630 W. Laskey Road
Toledo, OH 43612
419-476-2259
www.wessonbuilders.com

Clutter Busters

(These are generalists and do more than just organize garages.)

The people listed below do all different types of organizational projects. If you have a larger or more complex garage project, you may want to look for an organizer who specializes in garages, as they will most likely be more familiar with garage-specific products and trends.

Diane Campion
Organize This!
69 Woodside Drive
Albany, NY 12208
518-435-9948
www.Org-This.com

David Meester
Garage Detail
P.O. Box 1514
York, SC 29745
803-448-8273
www.garagedetail.com

Mary Mihaly
New Paradigms ~ Feng Shui
216-281-7270
www.marymihaly.com

Organizations

National Association of Professional Organizers (NAPO)
4700 West Lake Avenue
Glenview, IL 60025
847-375-4746
www.napo.net

This professional organization for organizers offers tips on selecting an organizer, a search engine for finding an organizer in your area, and tips on getting organized.

Index